Beadwork from North American Indian designs

Beadwork from North American Indian designs

Marjorie Murphy

B T Batsford Limited London

Colour photography
by Clive Boursnell

Line illustrations by Barbara Firth
Charts by George Dilks

First published 1974

ISBN 0 7134 2770 1

Filmset by Servis Filmsetting
Limited, Manchester
Printed and bound in
Great Britain by
William Clowes & Sons
Limited, Beccles, Suffolk
for the publishers
B T Batsford Limited
4 Fitzhardinge Street
London W1H 0AH

Contents

Acknowledgement

I should like to express my thanks to Mrs Vandall of White Rock, British Columbia, who introduced me to the craft of beadwork.

Portsmouth 1974 MM

Introduction

Beadwork has been used as a decorative craft for over three and a half thousand years, the earliest examples known being in Egypt. The craft has existed in Britain in primitive style, since the Bronze Age.

The beadwork in this book, although very different in the materials used, is nevertheless a development of these early beginnings. The North American Indian originally used bone, shells, and seeds as beads, but in the mid-fifteenth century, the introduction of glass beads from Europe encouraged the execution of many more intricate designs. The bead loom, now a modern product, was originally any convenient tree-branch, with the warp thread stretched tight by tying a rock on the end.

Although modern methods have superseded the old, many of the designs have retained the elements of tradition and mythology, and some of these traditional symbols, for example the 'Thunderbird', have been included in this book. The twentieth century has seen beadwork used extensively, for purses, bags, and even dresses, as well as in its usual form, for jewellery.

Here is an attempt to bring the techniques of this simple craft to the notice of people who are interested in the resurgence of hand crafts as a whole, and beadwork in particular. The descriptions of technique have been made as simple as the author could achieve and are intended for the use of school pupils as well as of adults. The designs are a mixture of traditional and modern elements and give a sound basis for future experiment with the craft.

Part 1 Basic stripwork

1 Materials and simple patterns

BEADS

All the samples illustrated are worked with 2/0 size of glass beads, known in the 'trade' as 'Rocaille'. This is, of course, with the exception of the wooden beads.

In the hand-worked necklaces, any size of bead, either glass, wooden, or chalk, can be used with extremely satisfying results.

It is recommended that sizes 2/0 or 3/0 glass beads are worked on the loom for the neatest result. However, a larger size of bead, glass or wooden, can be used to advantage. The use of wooden beads on the loom is described in Chapter 4.

LOOMS

It is possible to make one's own loom (Chapter 5). The one illustrated ensures a neat finish to one's work and is extremely simple to operate. The double rollers permit work of any length to be made and the warp threads are properly stretched and held in place without slipping. For the information of teachers and parents, this loom is as 'child-proof' as reasonably possible.

THREAD

Any synthetic thread can be used, but Coats *Drima* thread is particularly excellent for its combination of strength and thinness. Nylon thread is not recommended because of its stiffness.

A heavier thread may be used as warp on the loom where extra strength is required in the making of belts and similar items.

Shirring elastic as the warp thread on the loom will result in a well-elasticated beadwork strip suitable especially for a bracelet or child's hairband.

In all the beadwork patterns a great deal of thread is visible. It is therefore essential that the colour of the thread is matched to the colour of the beads. In the multicolour examples illustrated, black thread is used.

NEEDLES

Coates beading needles, size 10.

BEESWAX

Coating the thread with wax helps to prevent the thread tangling and gives extra strength.

A list of suppliers of all these materials can be found on page 94.

USEFUL RULES

1 Always thread the needle with a *long* thread. Double it and then run the thread twice through beeswax. This helps to strengthen the thread and prevents tangling.
2 Use a knot only at the very *beginning* of the necklace.
3 To illustrate each step clearly, all diagrams show a large gap between each bead. When making the necklaces, always pull the thread tightly to ensure that as little thread as possible is showing.
4 To ensure a good, even tension, always pull the thread tightly in the direction that it is going, and roll the beads between the finger and thumb to tighten the work.
5 Store the beads in oblong containers. The more beads in a container, the easier it is to pick them up.
6 To pick up the beads, hold the needle in a horizontal position, and run it through the beads. In a short time you will acquire the knack of scooping up just the correct number you need.
7 Marvellous effects can be obtained by using large beads, and even wooden ones. Instead of *Drima* thread, try using shirring elastic for pieces such as hairbands, or braclets.
8 It is advisable to work Patterns One and Two before attempting any of the other patterns included in the first two chapters.
9 Unless otherwise stated, start each pattern by making a knot 2 in. from the end of the double-waxed thread. Thread the first bead of the pattern and insert the needle between the two threads between the knot and the first bead. Pull tightly: Now commence the pattern. The 'tail' will later be threaded through a few beads before cutting.
10 To fasten off any necklace, work the needle through a few beads, make a slip knot (Chapter 3), and pass the needle through three more beads before cutting the thread.

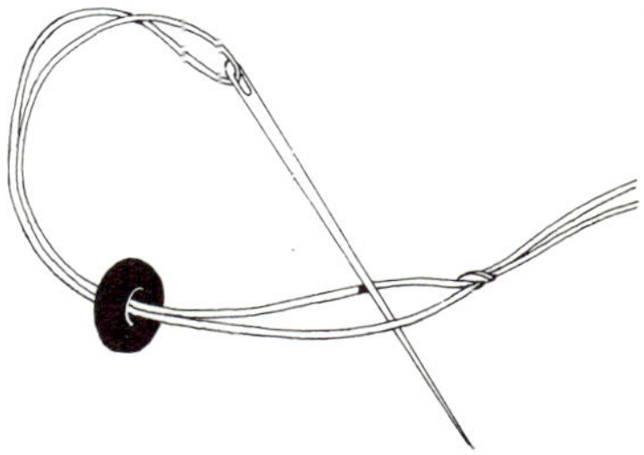

The first bead

PATTERN ONE A simple flower design.

Key

○ = outside bead (o)

● = bead forming zig-zag design (b)

Materials

2 ½-oz pkts beads (size optional)

2 beading needles, size 10

Drima thread

Beeswax

Thread the needle with a long thread. Double the thread and make a small knot near the end. Run the double thread twice through the beeswax to strengthen the thread and prevent tangles.

Start (see Chapter 3)

Pick up and thread 3b, 2o, 3b. Make a circle by inserting the needle between the two threads in the interval between the knot and the beads. Pull tightly.

1

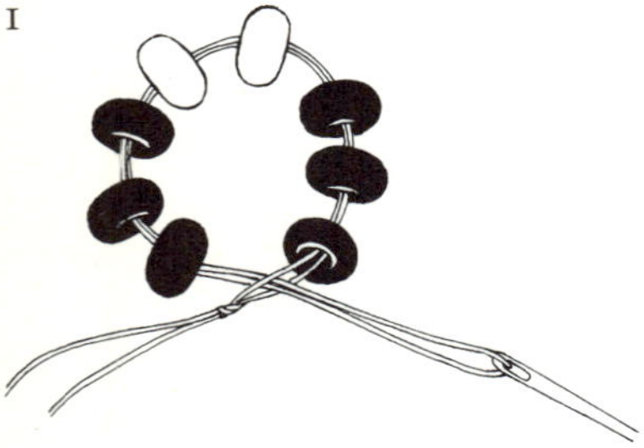

Pattern

Pick up and thread 2o, 3b, and pass the needle through the third b.

2

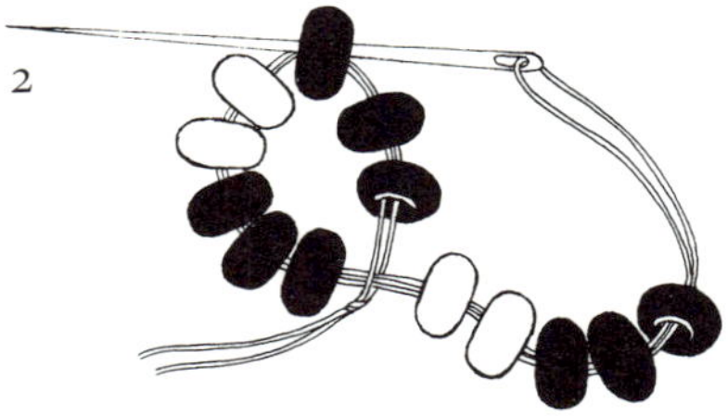

3

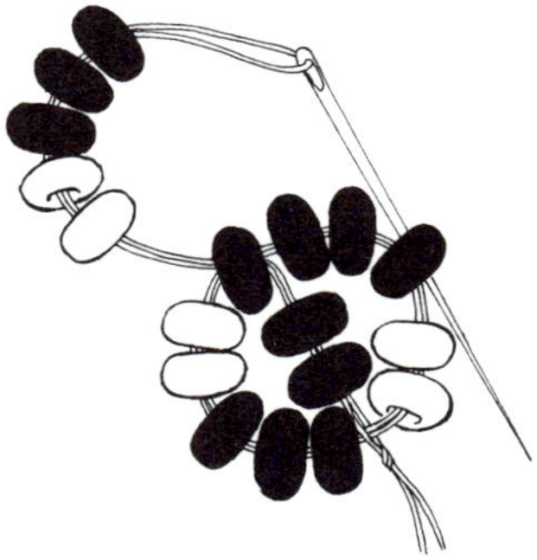

Repeat the pattern until the desired length is achieved. For ways to renew the thread and to finish the necklace, see Chapter 3.

PATTERN TWO This flower design can be varied to make many necklaces.

Key

● = petals (p)
○ = centre (c)

Materials

1 1-oz pkt beads (size optional)
A few beads of contrasting colour for centres
2 beading needles, size 10
Drima thread
Beeswax

Start

Pick up and thread 6p. Make a circle by inserting the needle between the two threads in the interval between the knot and the beads. Pull tightly.
Thread 1c and pass needle through the 4th bead of the circle. Pull tightly, pressing bead c into the centre of the circle.

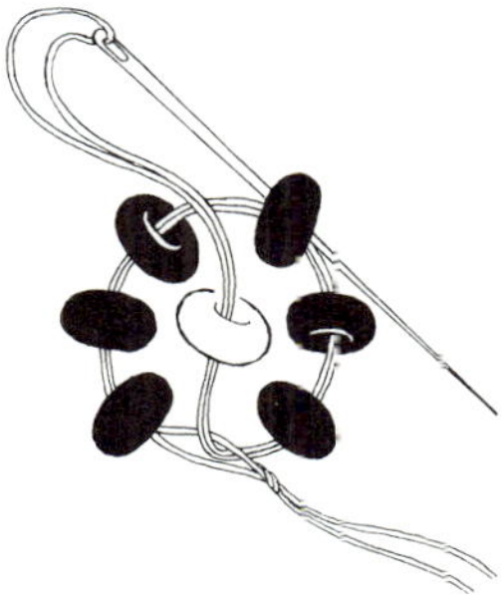

Pattern

1 Thread 2p, 1c, and pass the needle through the bead next to the bead out of which the thread comes.
2 Thread 2p and pass the needle through bead p next to centre bead c. Pull tightly.

1

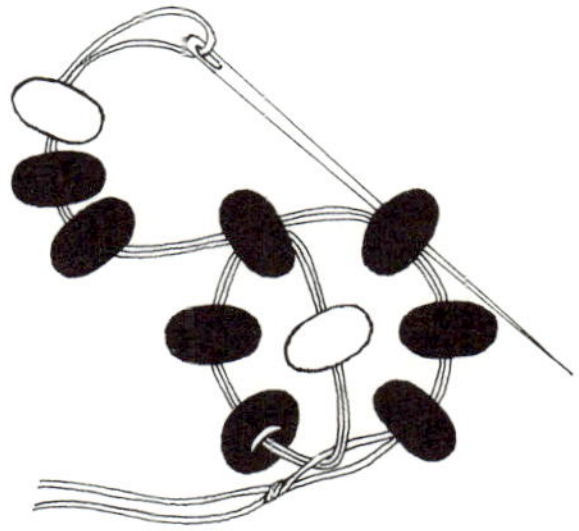

2

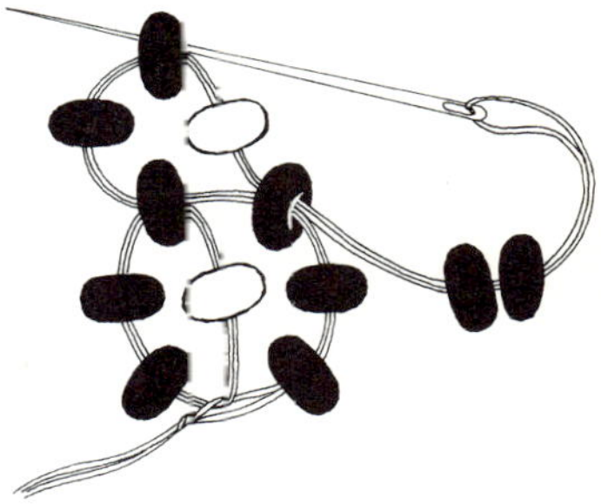

Repeat stages 1 and 2 until desired length is achieved.
For ways to renew the thread and to finish the necklace, see Chapter 3.

PATTERN THREE A variation on a floral design.

Key

● = petals (p)

○ = centre and part of chain (c)

⊙ = centre part of chain (x)

Materials

2 ½-oz pkts beads } size
1 ¼-oz pkt beads } optional
2 beading needles
Drima thread
Beeswax

The flower is the same as in Pattern Two.

Start

Pick up and thread 6p. Make a circle. Thread 1c and pass the needle through the 4th bead of the circle. Pull tightly, pressing bead c into the centre of the circle.

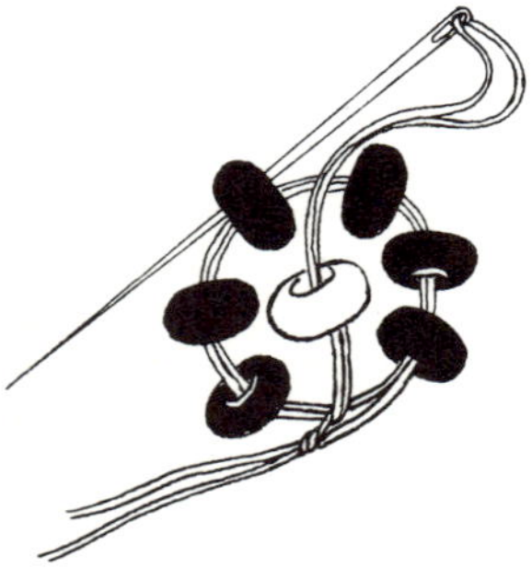

Thread 3c, 8x, 3c, 2p, 3c, 8x, 3c (ps are petals for next flower.) Pass the needle through the top two petals of the flower to come out the same bead as the thread.

1

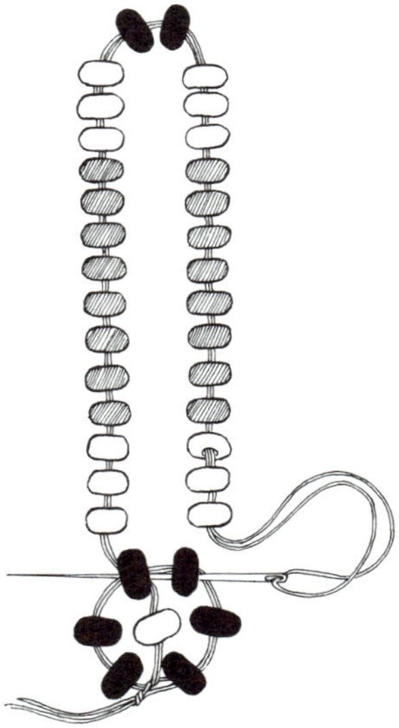

Pass the needle up again through 3c, 8x, 3c, and make another flower as follows:
Thread 2p, 1c, and pass through bead as in diagram.

2

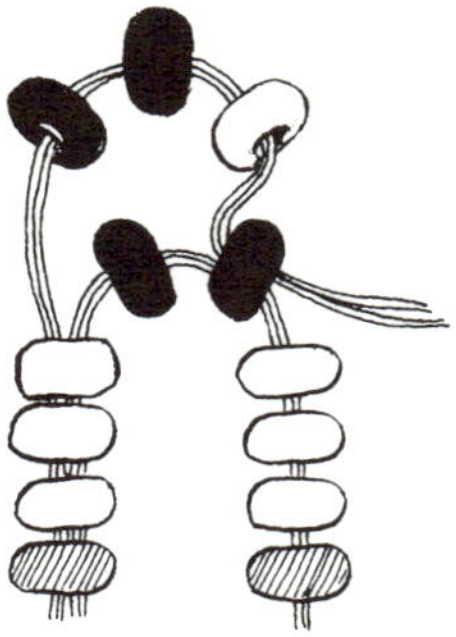

Thread 2p, and pass the needle through bead p, next to centre bead c. Pull tightly.

3

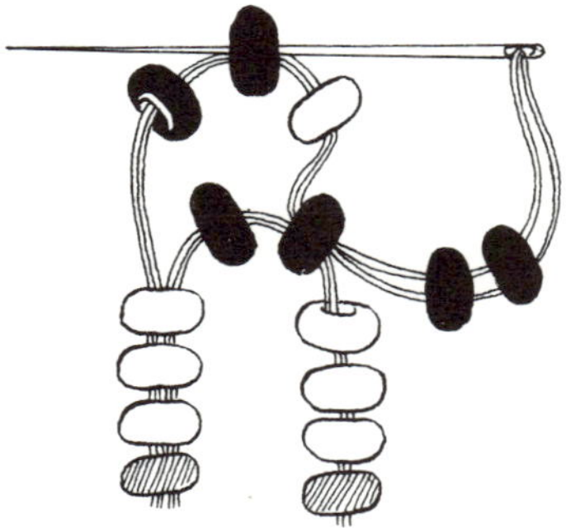

Continue until desired length is reached. (To renew thread, see Chapter 3.)
The two most popular methods for finishing a necklace are illustrated in Chapter 3.
Another attractive ending is made by joining the two ends with the basic flower and then fringing.

PATTERN FOUR This pattern is suitable for a child.

Key
○ = petals (p)
● = centre and connecting 'rope' of beads (c)

Materials
2 ½-oz pkts beads (size optional)
2 beading needles
Drima thread
Beeswax

Start
Thread 6p, and make a circle. Thread 1c and pass the needle through the 4th bead of the circle. Pull tightly pressing bead c into the centre of the circle.

Pattern
1 Thread 9c, 4p, 1c, and pass needle through first bead p.
2 Add 2p, and pass the needle through bead p, next to bead c.
Continue working the two stages of the pattern until the desired length is achieved.
For ways to renew the thread and to finish the pattern, see Chapter 3.

1

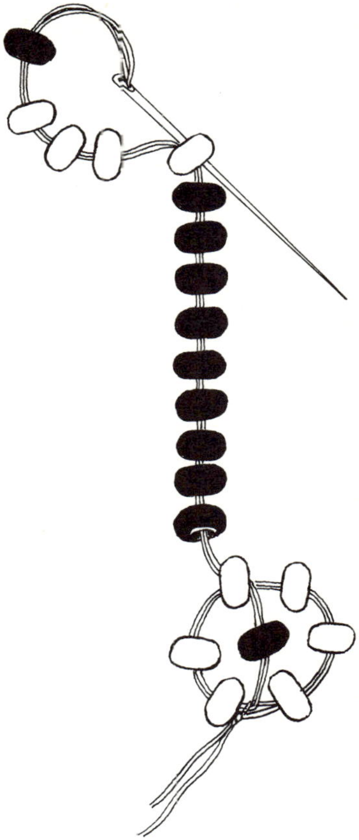

2

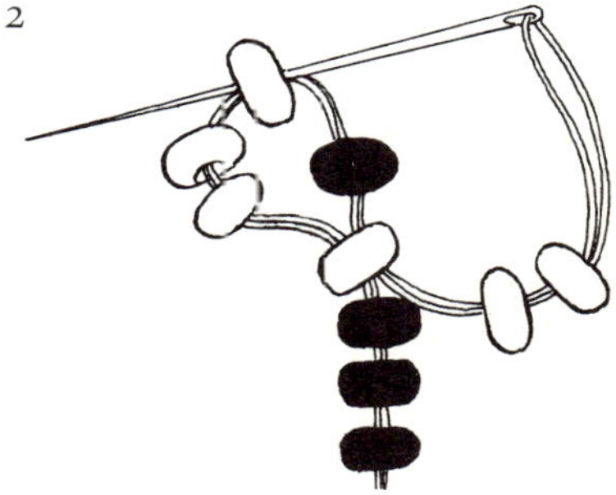

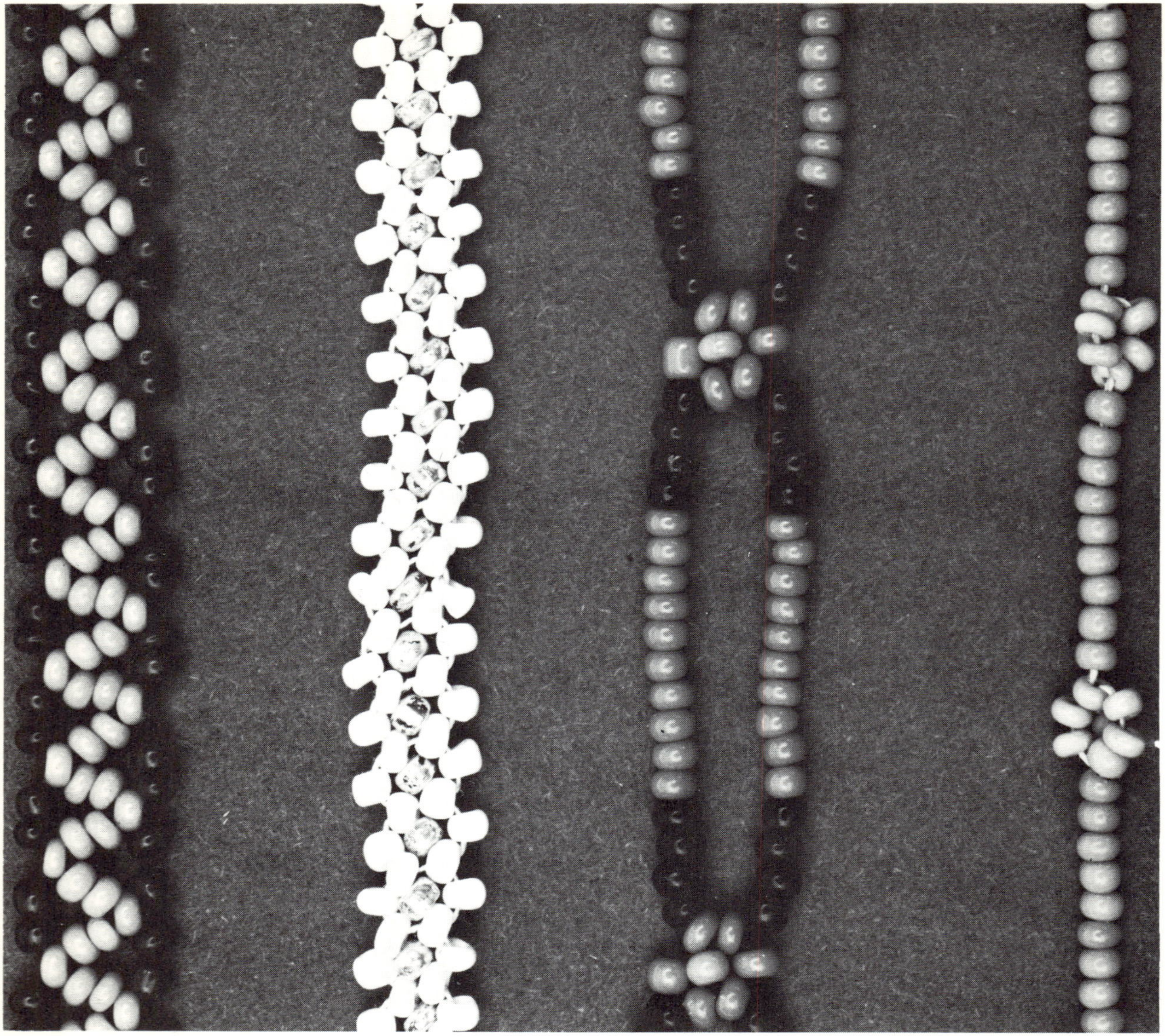

(*left to right*): Patterns 1, 2, 3 and 4

2a More intricate designs

PATTERN FIVE Another basic flower with two centres.

Key
○ = petals (p)
● = centre (c)

Materials
1 1-oz pkt beads (size optional)
A few beads of contrasting colour
2 beading needles
Drima thread
Beeswax

Start
Thread 8p, and make a circle. Add 2c, and pass the needle through the fifth p.
Pull tightly.

1

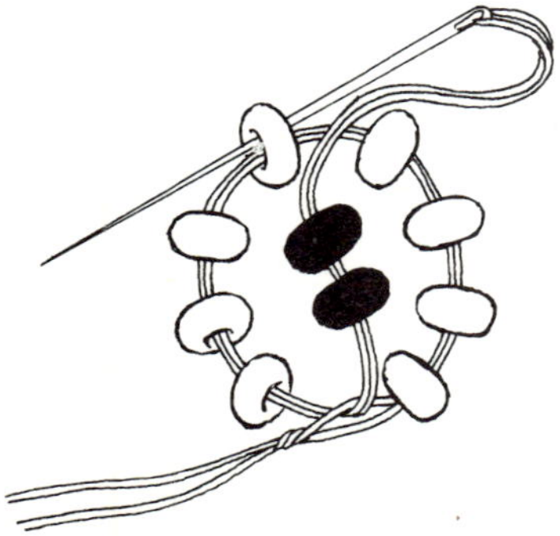

Pattern
Thread 3p, 2c, and pass the needle through the next bead p.

2

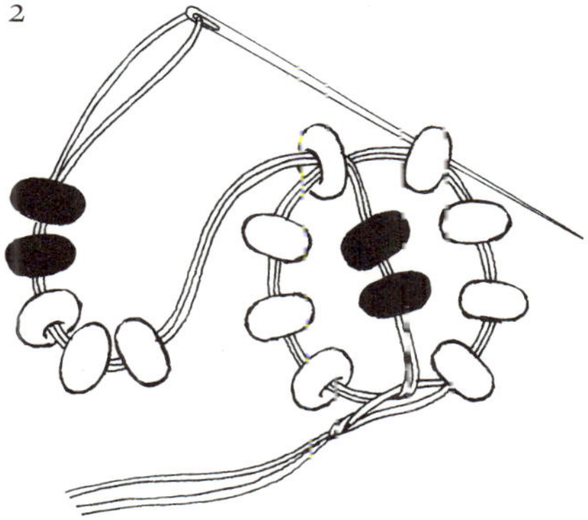

Thread 3p, and pass the needle through bead p, next to bead c. Continue in pattern until desired length is reached.

3

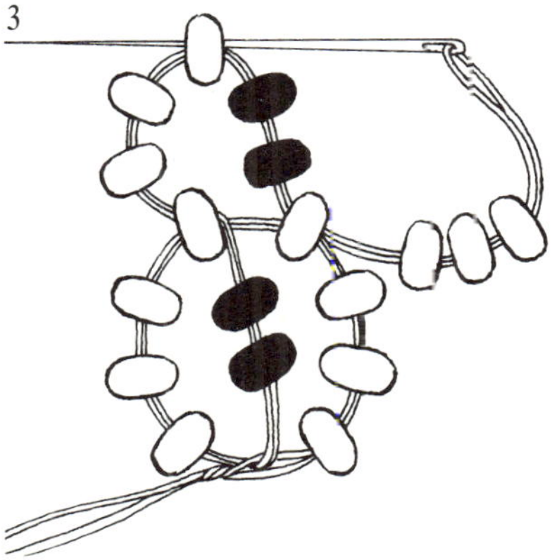

For ways to renew the thread and to finish the pattern, see Chapter 3.

PATTERN SIX Floral patterns can be made using alternating colours.

Key

○ = first colour (p)

● = contrast colour (c)

Materials

1 $\frac{1}{2}$-oz pkt beads (size optional)

1 $\frac{1}{2}$-oz pkt contrast colour (size optional)

2 beading needles

Drima thread

Beeswax

Start

Thread 8p, and make a circle. Add 1c, and pass the needle through the fifth bead, and press bead c, into the centre of the circle.

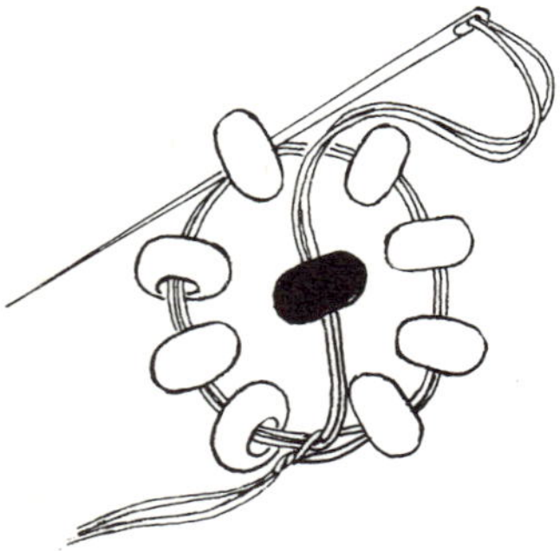

Pattern

1 Thread 2c, and pass the needle through the two top p.

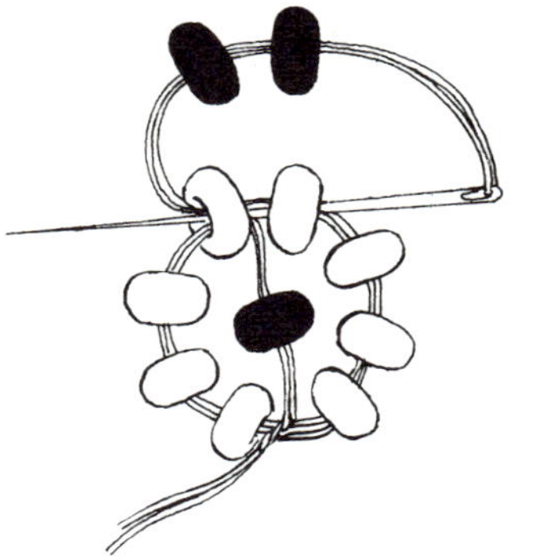

Pass the needle up through 1c. Pull tightly.

2 Thread 1p, 3c, and pass the needle through 2c. Pull tightly.

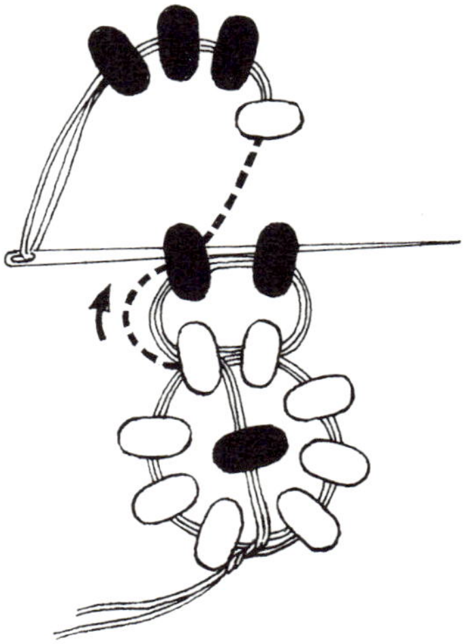

Thread 3c, and pass the needle through the first c, next to the centre bead p. Pull tightly.

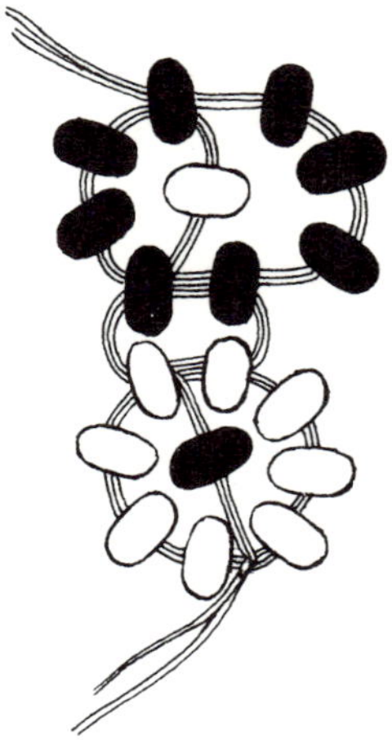

3 Thread 2p, and pass the needle through the two top c. Pass the needle up through 1p. Pull tightly.

4 Thread 1c, 3p, and pass the needle through 2p. Pull tightly. Thread 3p, and pass the needle through the first p, next to the centre bead c. Pull tightly.

Continue stages 1, 2, 3 and 4 until desired length is achieved. Remember to alternate colours when starting a new flower. For ways to renew thread and to finish the necklace, see Chapter 3.

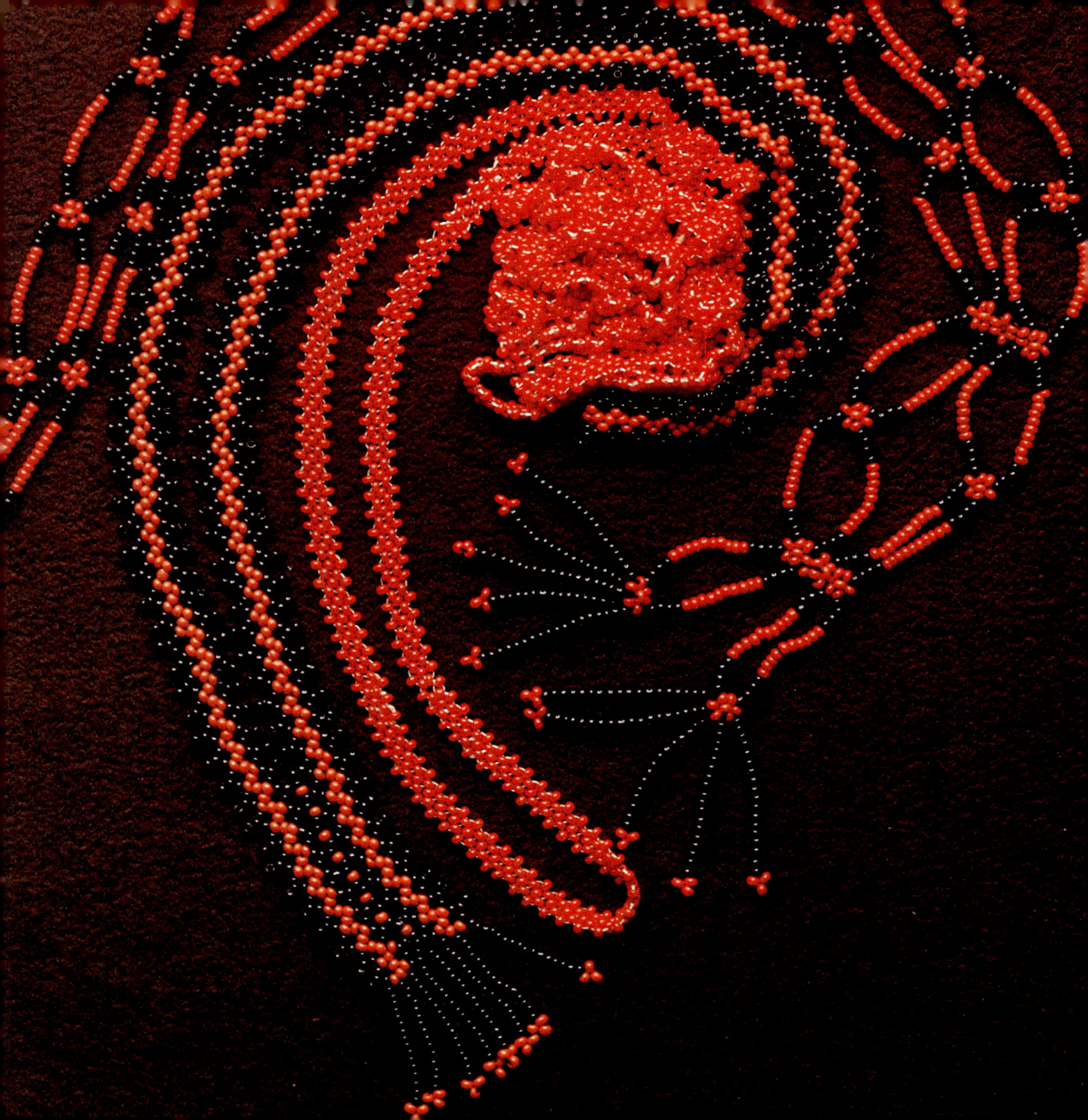

PATTERN SEVEN This pattern, known as the arrow design is worked in two colours.

Key

● = first colour (p)
○ = contrast colour (c)

Materials

1 ½-oz pkt beads
1 ½-oz pkt beads of contrasting colour (size optional)
2 beading needles
Drima thread
Beeswax

Start

Pick up and thread 6p. Make a circle. Thread 1p, and pass the needle through the fourth bead of the circle. Pull tightly, pressing the bead into the centre of the circle.

Pattern

1 Thread 2c, 1p and pass the needle through the bead next to the bead out of which the thread comes.

1

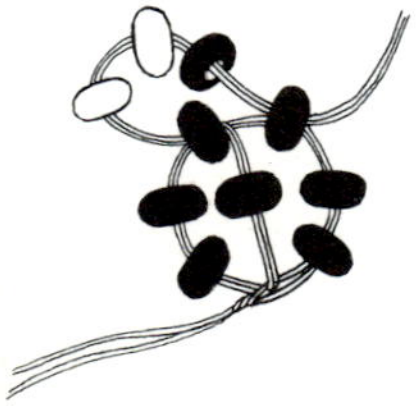

Thread 2c, and pass the needle through the bead c, next to the centre bead p.
Thread 3c, and pass through the bead next to the bead out of which the thread comes.

2

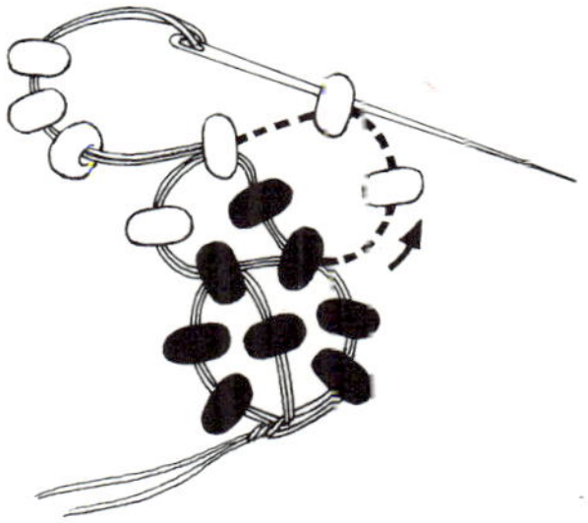

Thread 2c, and pass through the middle of the three just picked up.
Pick up 2p, 1c and work through bead, pick up 2p.

3

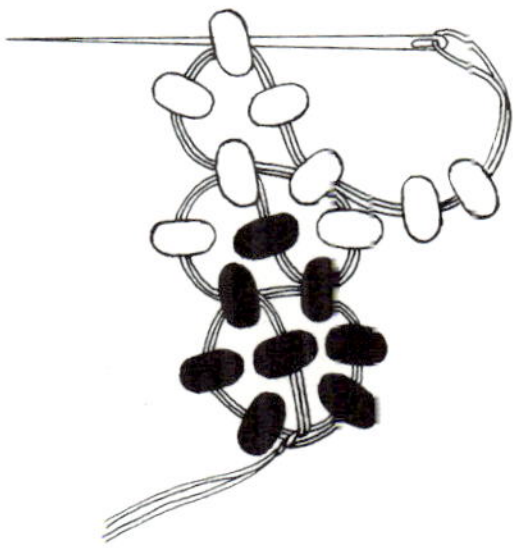

Continue making the basic flower but use the colours stated in the *next* stage.

2 Pick up 3p, work through bead, pick up 2p. Pick up 2c, 1p, work through bead, pick up 2c. Pick up 3c, work through bead, pick up 2c. Pick up 2p, 1c, and work through bead, pick up 2p.

Repeat stage 2 until the necklace is the desired length.
For ways to renew thread and to finish the necklace, see Chapter 3.

Colour plate, opposite:
(*left to right*); Patterns 11, 7 and 3
(*reading at below centre*)

PATTERN EIGHT This is the basic floral design with an attractive coloured flower worked after each group of sixteen flowers.

Key

○ = petals (p)
⊙ = leaves (v)
● = petals of coloured flower (pc)
⊗ = centre of coloured flower (cc)

Materials

1 1-oz pkt beads (size optional)
A few beads for contrast (size optional)
2 beading needles
Drima thread
Beeswax

Start

Thread 6p, and make a circle. Add 1p, and pass the needle through the fourth bead p, pressing bead p, into the centre. Work 8 basic flowers using beads p for *all* petals and centres. (See Pattern Two.)

To make coloured flower

Still continue basic flower but substitute colours as follows:

★1 Thread 1p, 1 leaf bead v, 1p, and pass the needle through the next bead.

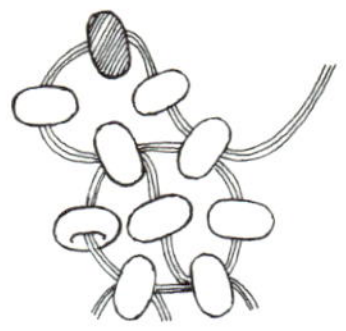

Thread 2p, and pass the needle through the leaf bead v. Pull tightly.

2 Thread 1p, 1pc, 1v, and pass the needle through bead p next to bead v.

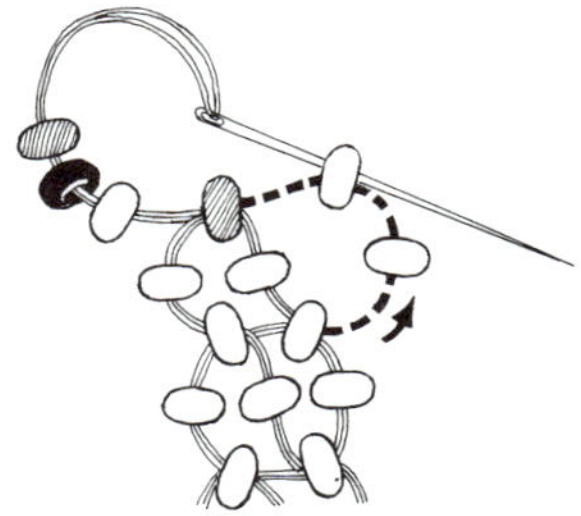

Add 1p, 1pc and pass the needle through the petal bead pc next to the leaf bead v.

3 Add 2pc, 1cc, and pass the needle through the next bead pc.

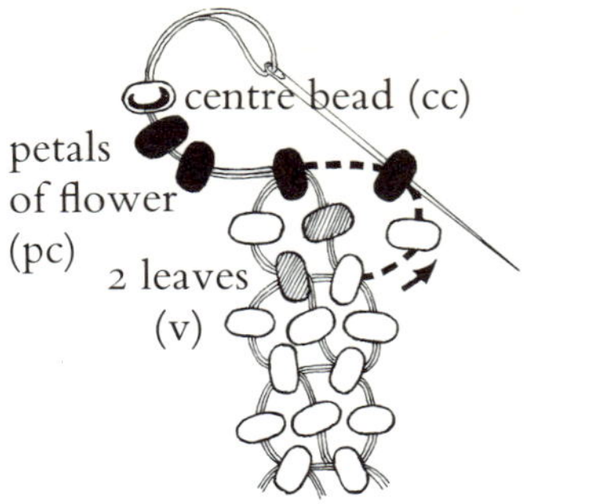

4 Add 2pc and pass the needle through the pc bead next to bead cc. You have now completed the flower. The remaining leaves will be worked in the following flower.

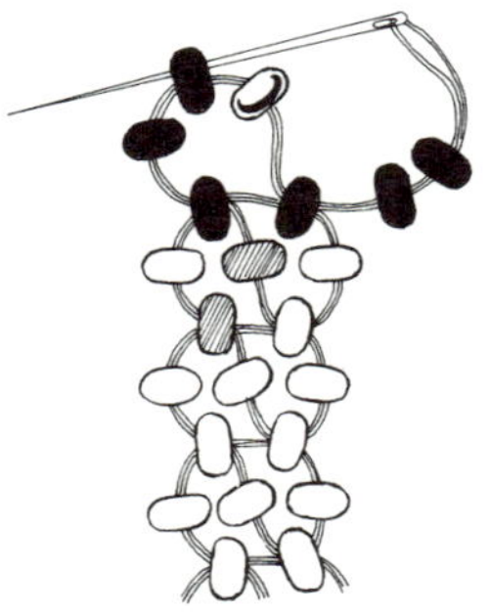

5 Thread 2p, 1v and pass the needle through the next bead pc.
Thread 1p, 1v and pass the needle through bead p, next to the leaf bead v.
★

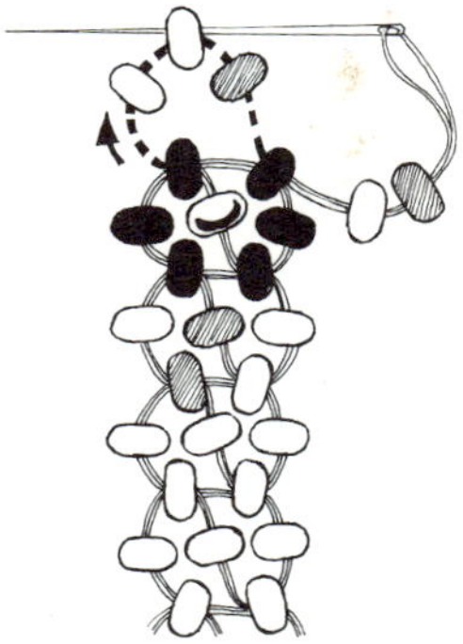

You have now fully completed the coloured flower and its leaves.
Work 16 basic flowers with beads p and then repeat coloured flower, ★ to ★.
Continue in pattern until desired length is achieved.
For ways to renew the thread and to finish the pattern see Chapter 3.

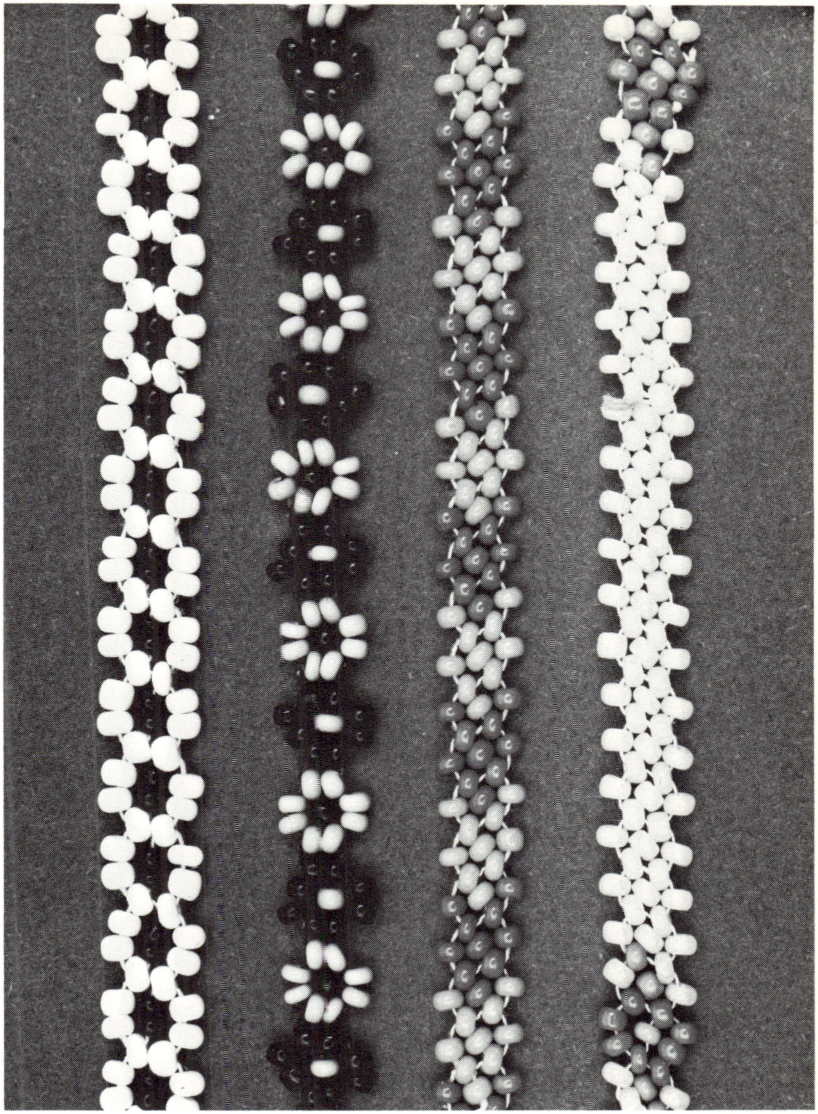

(*left to right*): Patterns 5, 6, 7 and 8

PATTERN NINE This is for flowers with four beads in each centre.

Key

○ = petals (p)

● = centres (c)

Materials

1 $\frac{1}{2}$-oz pkt beads

1 $\frac{1}{2}$-oz pkt contrast beads (size optional)

2 beading needles

Drima thread

Beeswax

Start

Pick up and thread 2p, 2c, 2p, and make a circle in the usual way. Pull tightly. Thread 1c, and pass the needle through 1c, and pull tightly, pressing the bead c into the centre.

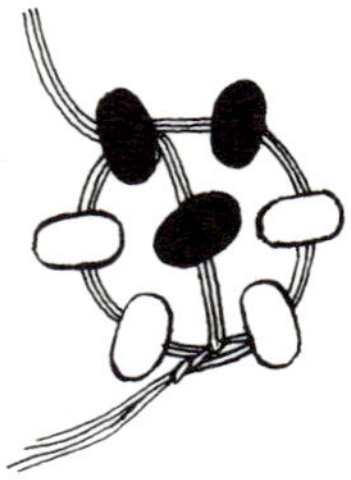

From now on work the flowers as in Pattern Two. Pick up and thread 2p, 1c, and pass the needle through bead c, next to bead out of which the thread comes. Pull tightly.

Pick up and thread 2p, and pass the needle back through bead p, next to bead c. Pull tightly.

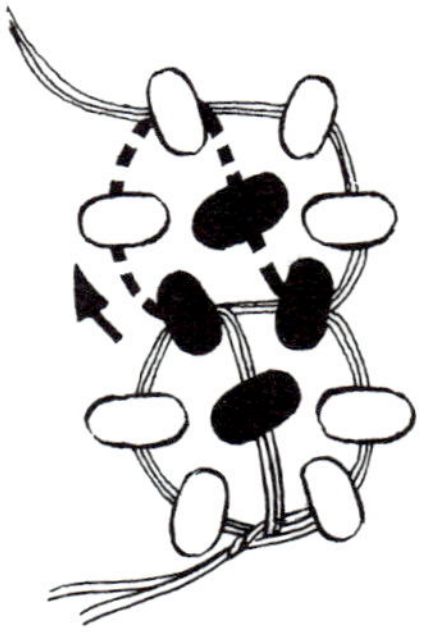

Pattern

1 Pick up 1p, 2c, and pass through bead p, next to bead p, out of which the thread comes.

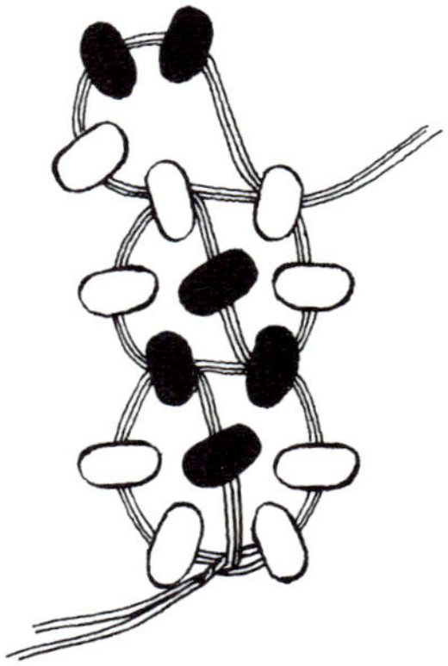

2 Pick up 1p, 1c and pass the needle back through bead c.

3 Pick up 2p, 1c, and pass through bead c, as illustrated. Pull tightly.

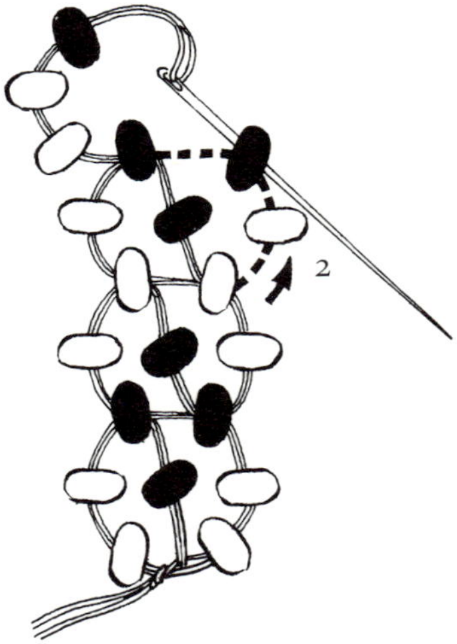

4 Pick up 2p, and pass through bead p, next to bead c. Pull tightly.

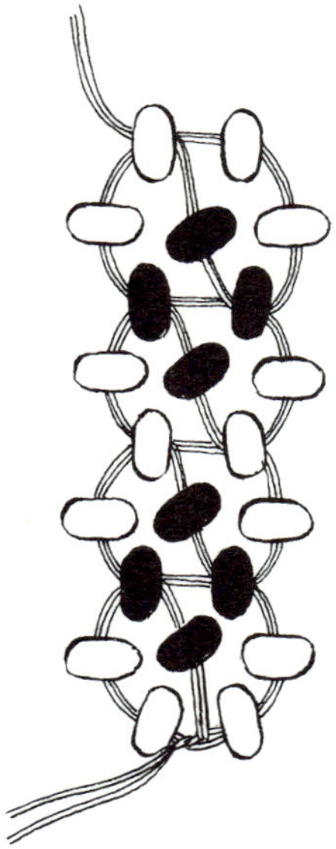

The second flower is now complete. Continue the four stages of the pattern until the desired length is achieved.
For ways to renew thread and to finish the necklace, see Chapter 3.

PATTERN TEN This is known as the Bar stitch.

Key
○ = petals and centres (p)
● = 'bar' beads (b)

Materials
1 $\frac{1}{2}$-oz pkt beads
Sufficient beads for 'bar' (size optional)
2 beading needles
Drima thread
Beeswax

Start
Thread 6p, and make a circle. Add one bead p, and pass the needle through the fourth bead p. Pull tightly, pressing bead p into the centre.

Pattern
1 Thread 1b, 1p, 1b, and pass the needle through bead as illustrated.

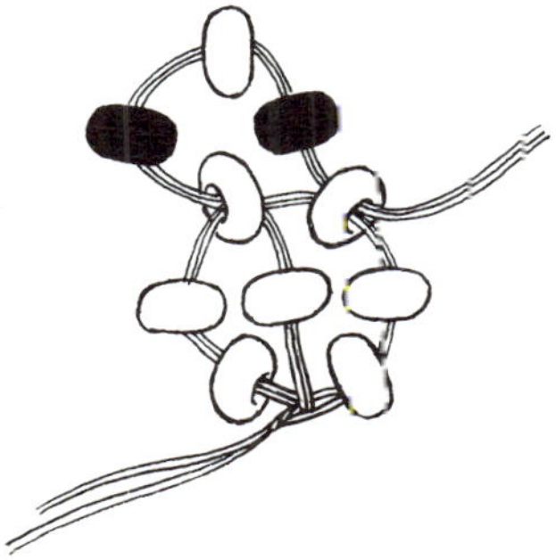

2 Thread 1b, 1p, and pass the needle through bead b, as illustrated.

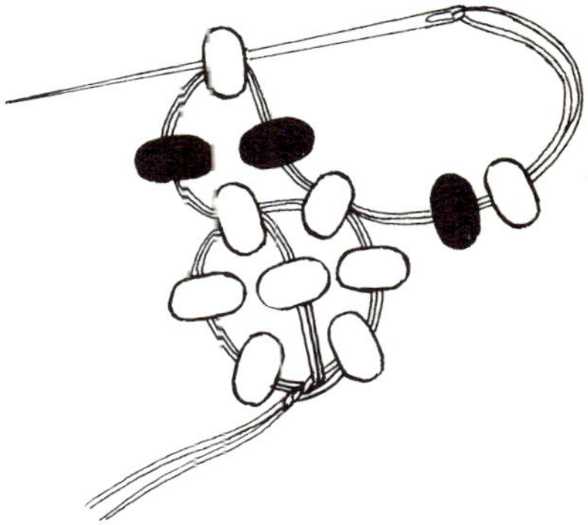

3 Work one basic flower as in Pattern Two, using beads p.
Repeat the three stages of the pattern until the desired length is achieved.

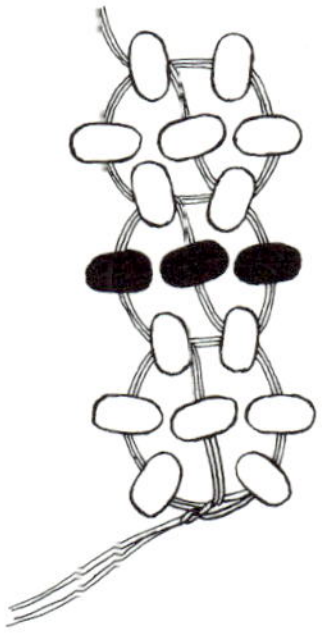

For ways to renew thread and to finish the necklace, see Chapter 3.

PATTERN ELEVEN A diamond pattern offers many possibilities.

Materials

1 1-oz pkt beads (size optional)
2 beading needles
Drima thread
Beeswax

Start

a Thread 8 beads and pass the needle back through no. 7 bead.
b Thread three beads.
c Pass the needle through the fourth bead.
d Thread three beads.
e Pass the needle back through the middle bead of the three just threaded.
f Thread three beads and pass the needle through the fourth bead from the top.
g Turn the chain over and bead will be in position of fig. d. Work from d to g for desired length.

For ways to renew thread and to finish the necklace see Chapter 3.

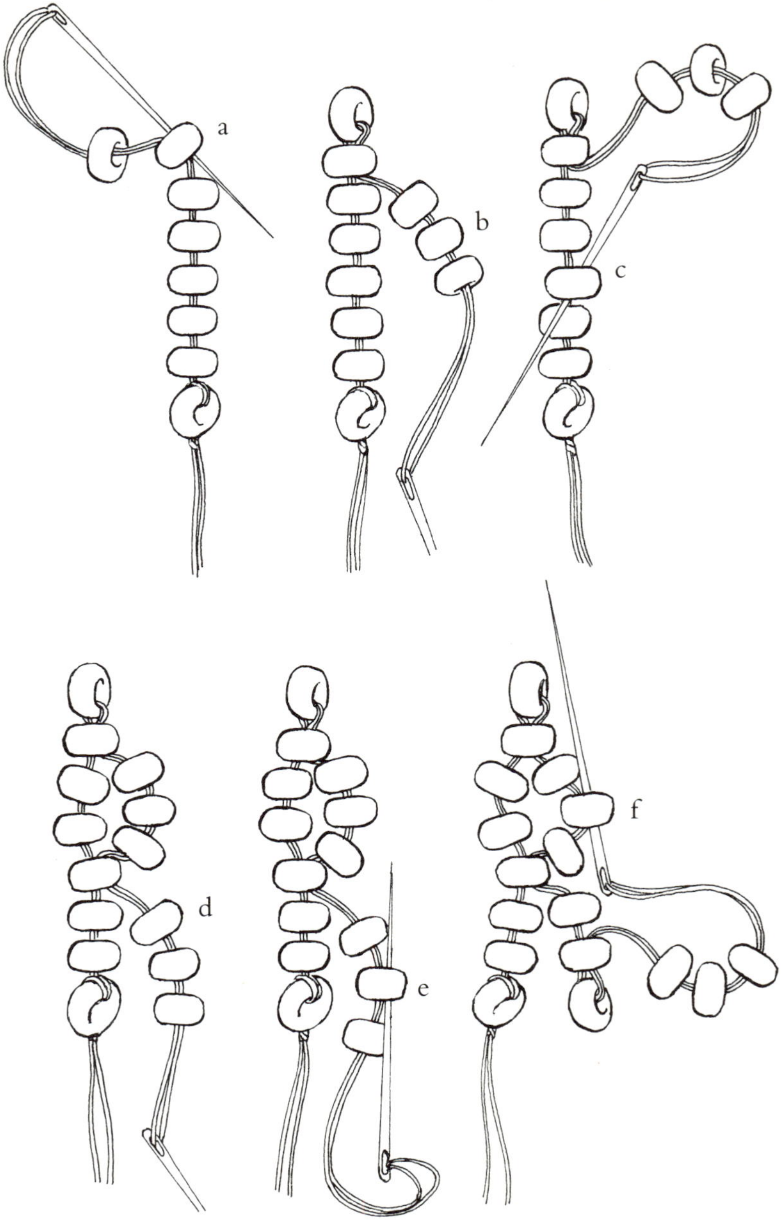

Here is an interesting variation

Key

○ = beads for the edges (p)
● = beads for the centre zig-zag (c)

Materials

1 $\frac{1}{2}$-oz pkt beads (size optional)
1 $\frac{1}{2}$-oz pkt contrasting beads (size optional)
2 Beading needles
Drima thread
Beeswax

Follow the pattern as described above, but vary the colour of the beads used, for example:

a 3p, 2c, 3p.
b 1p, 2c.
d 3p.
f 1p, 2c.

PATTERN TWELVE This 'chain' design looks very attractive if two colours are used. For example: three chains in the first colour and three chains in the second colour.

Materials

1 $\frac{1}{2}$-oz pkt beads (size optional)
2 beading needles
Drima thread
Beeswax

Start

Pick up and thread 8 beads. Make a circle by inserting the needle between the two threads between the knot at the end and the first bead. Pull tightly. Pass the needle up two beads and commence pattern as follows:

Pattern

★Thread 6 beads and pass the needle through the top two beads of the previous circle. Pull tightly.

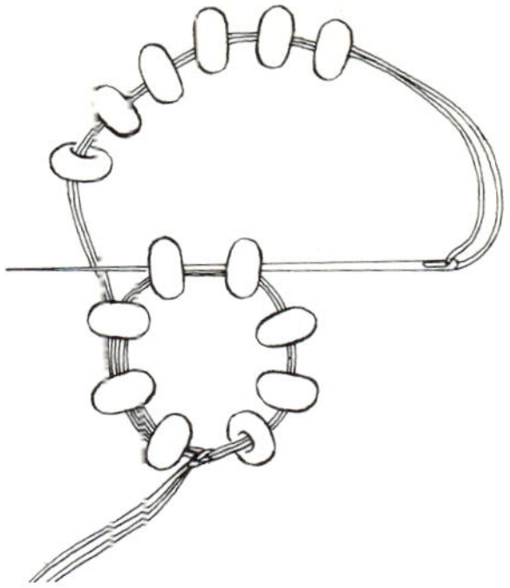

Pass the needle up 2 beads of the newly-formed circle.★

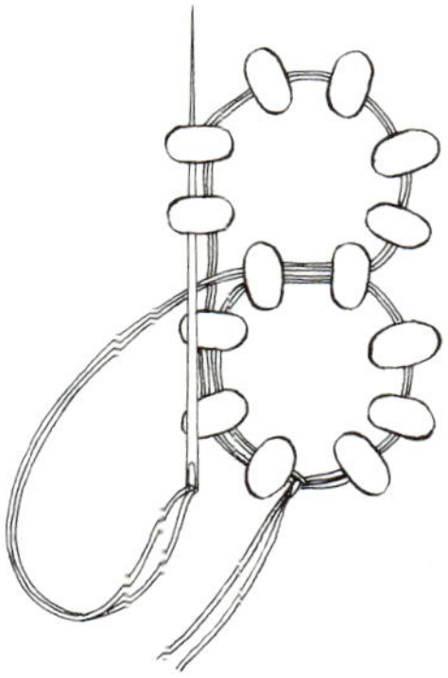

Repeat from ★ to ★ until the desired length is achieved. For ways to renew thread and to finish the necklace, see Chapter 3.

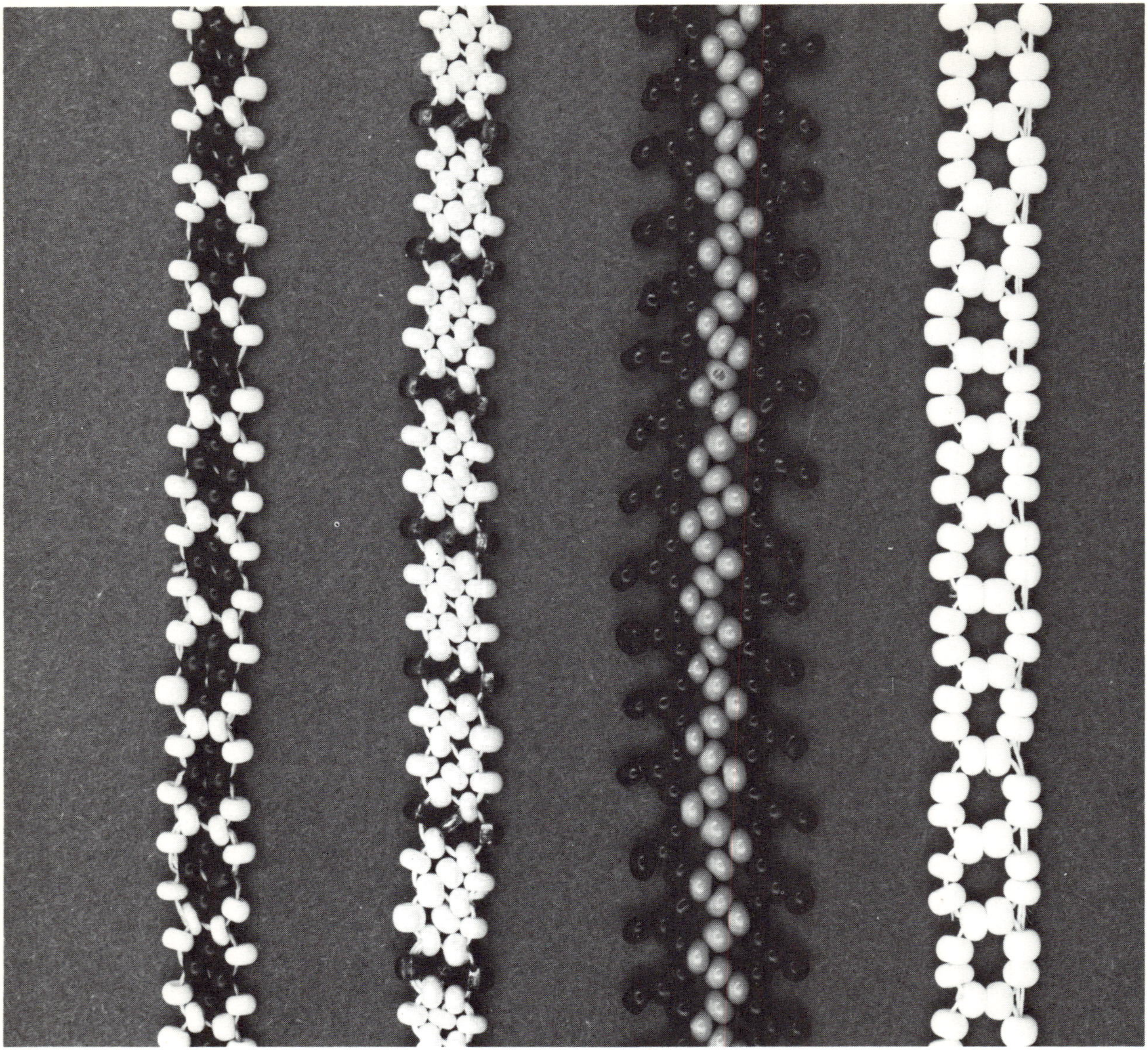

(*left to right*): Patterns 9, 10, 11 and 12

2b Collar designs and variations

PATTERN THIRTEEN A collar necklace.

Key

● = main colour (m)

○ = contrast colour (c)

Materials

1 $\frac{1}{2}$-oz pkt beads for main colour

1 $\frac{1}{4}$-oz pkt beads for contrast colour

2 beading needles

Beeswax

Start

1 Thread 1c, 5m, 1c, 5m, 1c, 5m, 2c.

2 Pass the needle through the second bead c.

3 Thread 5m, 1c, 5m, and pass the needle through the 2nd bead c down.

4 Thread 5m, 1c, 5m, 1c, 5m, and pass the needle through bead c.

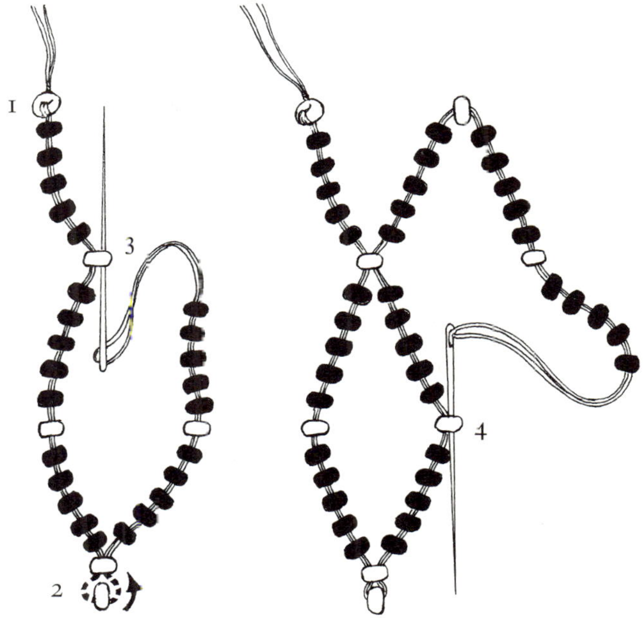

5 Thread 5m, 2c, and work through the second bead.

6 Thread 5m, 1c, 5m, and pass the needle through bead c. Repeat 4, 5, and 6 until the desired length is worked. This is usually 48 points.

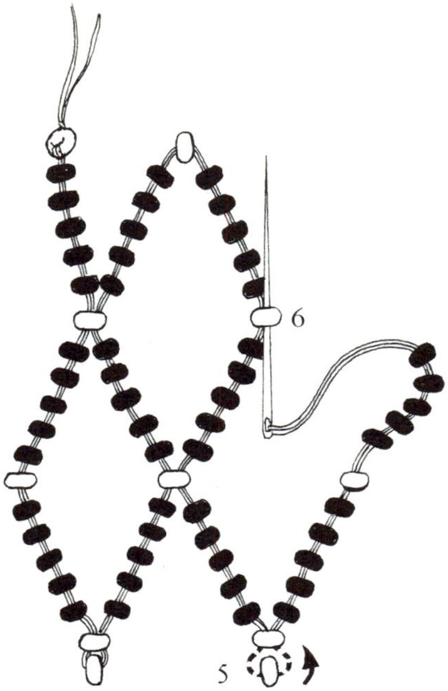

Finish

Sew all the top contrasts together using 4 beads m between each bead c. The necklace can be fastened either with a velvet ribbon caught through the necklace ends and tied, or with the aid of a barrel-type clasp fastener sewn on to each end. These clasp fasteners are available from most haberdashery departments.

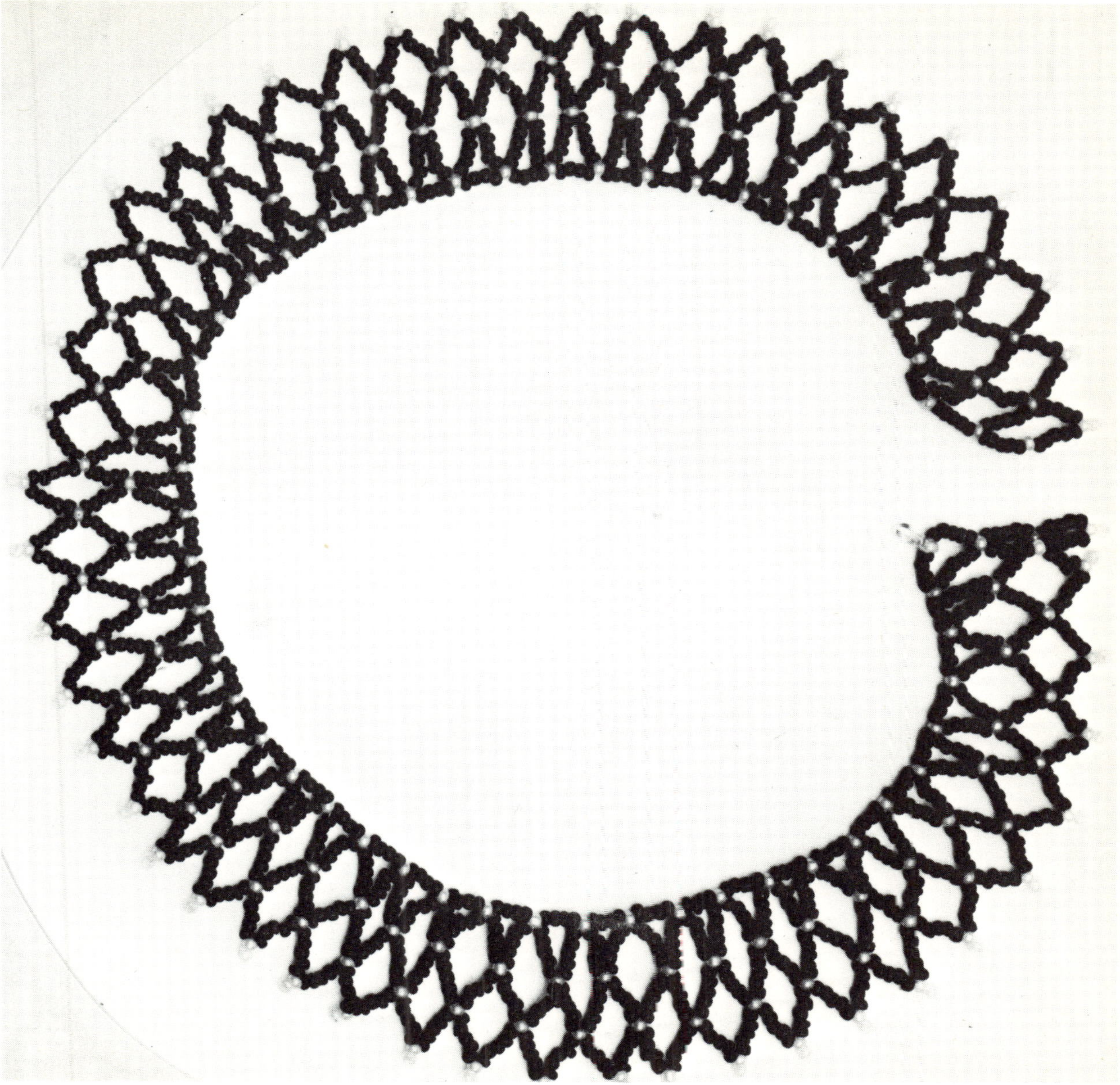

PATTERN FOURTEEN A beaded collar.

Materials

1 $\frac{1}{2}$-oz pkt beads for main colour (size 2/0 glass beads were used in the illustration)
1 $\frac{1}{2}$-oz pkt bugle beads
1 $\frac{1}{4}$-oz pkt beads for contrast colour
2 beading needles
Drima thread
Beeswax

Start

Thread a needle with a long thread. Double and wax it. Make a small knot 2 in. from the end. (The 'tail' will later be threaded into the beadwork before it is cut off).
Thread one contrast bead and pass the needle between the two threads between the knot and the bead. Pull tightly.

Key

● = contrast bead (c)
▭ = bugle bead (b)
○ = main colour (m)

Pattern

1 Firstly, thread 2b, 1c, 4m, 1c, 4m, 1c, 5m, 1c, 5m, 1c, 2b, 1m, 1c, 1m, 2b, 1c, 20m, 1c, 2b, 1m.
2 Pass the needle through the contrast bead.
3 Add 1m, 2b, 1c, 5m, and pass the needle through the contrast bead.
4 Add 5m, 1c, 4m, and pass the needle through the contrast bead.
5 Add 4m, 1c, 2b, and pass through the contrast bead.
6 Add 4m, 1c, 2b, and pass the needle through the contrast bead.

Continue in this way for the desired length. Pass the needle through the last few beads and secure with a slip knot (see Chapter 3).
Thread the needle through two more beads and cut the thread.
Attach the fastenings (see Chapter 3).

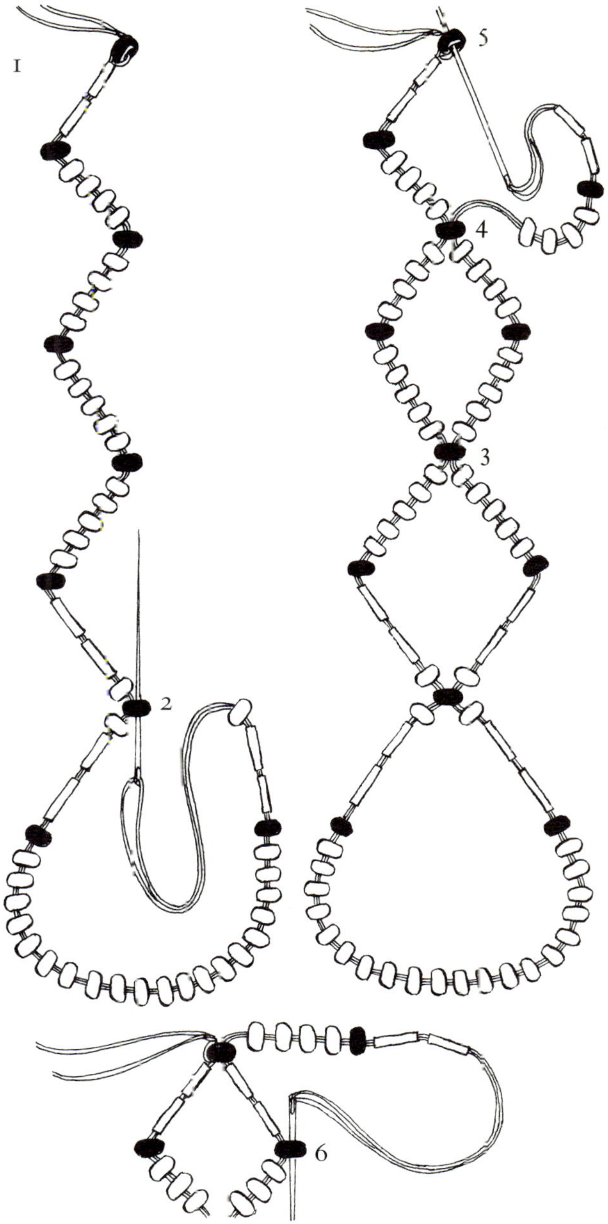
1
2
5
4
3
6

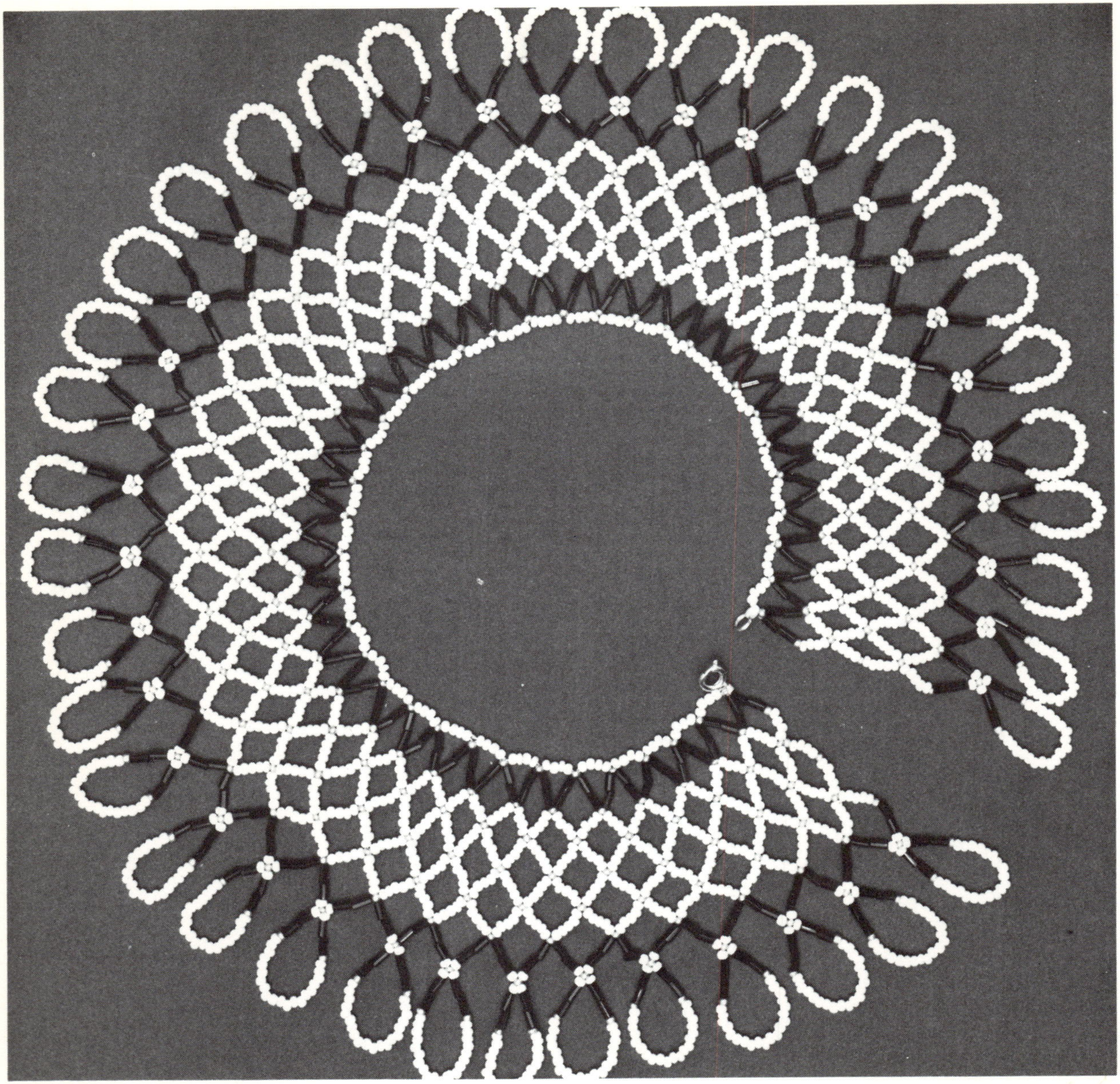

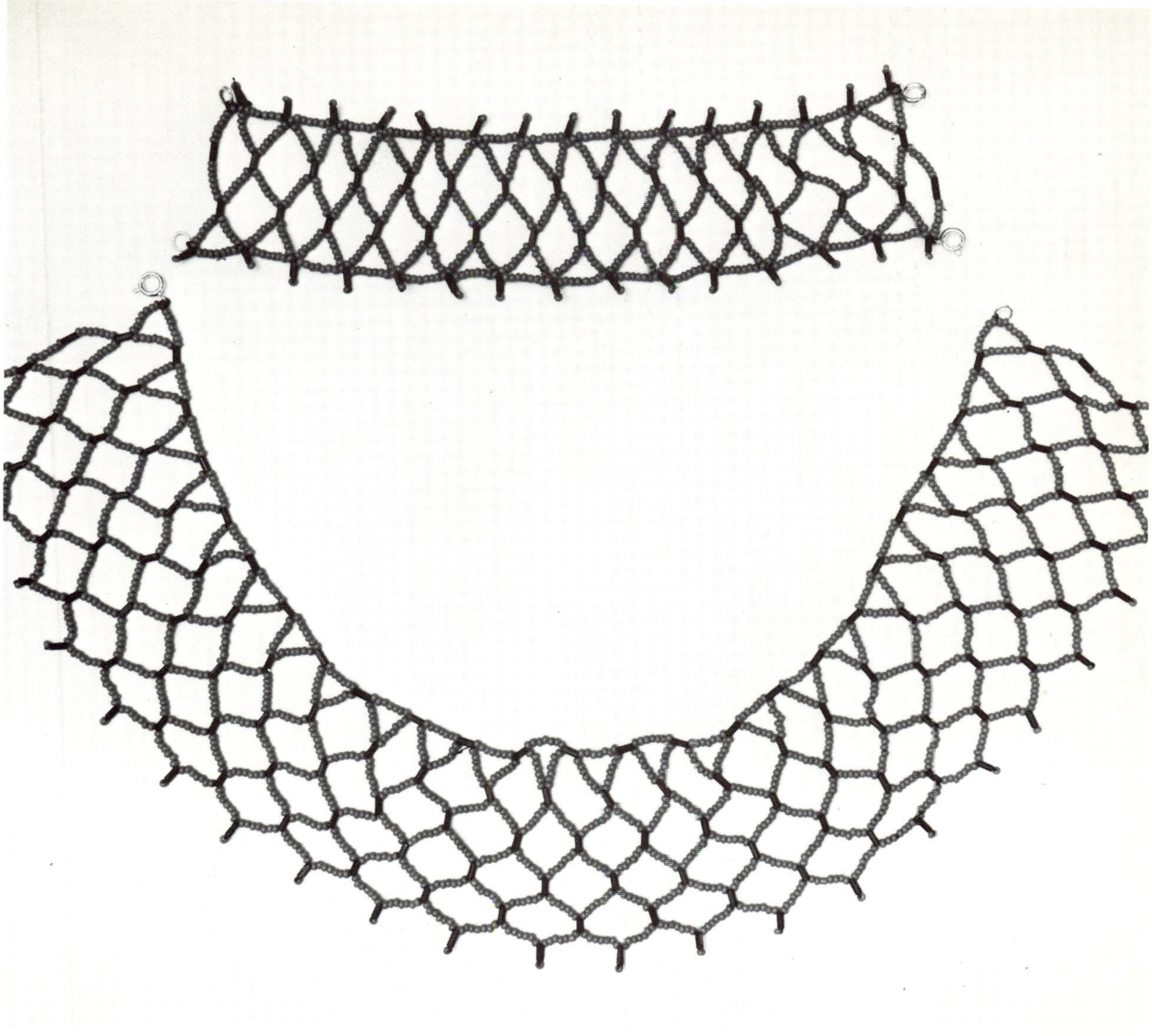

(*left and right*): Patterns 14 and 15

PATTERN FIFTEEN Beaded collar with matching bracelet.

Materials
2 1-oz pkt beads for main colour (size optional)
1 1-oz bugle beads for contrast
2 Beading needles
Drima thread
Beeswax.

Key
○ = main colour (m)
— = contrast colour (bugle bead) (c)

The collar pattern
Thread a needle with a long double thread. Wax it. Thread 7m, 1c, forty times or until the required neck-length is reached. End with 8m. Pass the needle back through the next to the last bead to secure the thread and then commence the pattern as follows:

1 Pick up and thread 7m, 1c, 7m, 1c, 7m, 1c, 7m, 1c, 7m, 1c, 1m. Make a 'prong' by passing the needle back through the contrast bead.
2 Pick up and thread 7m, 1c, 7m, and pass the needle through the second contrast bead up from the prong.

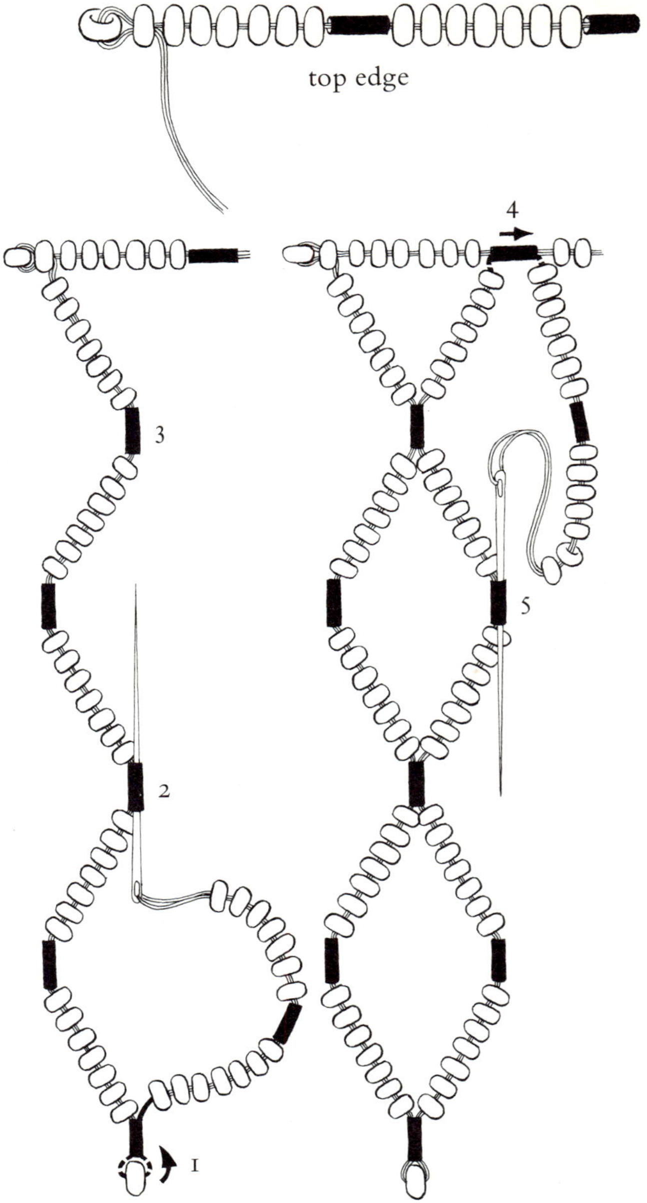

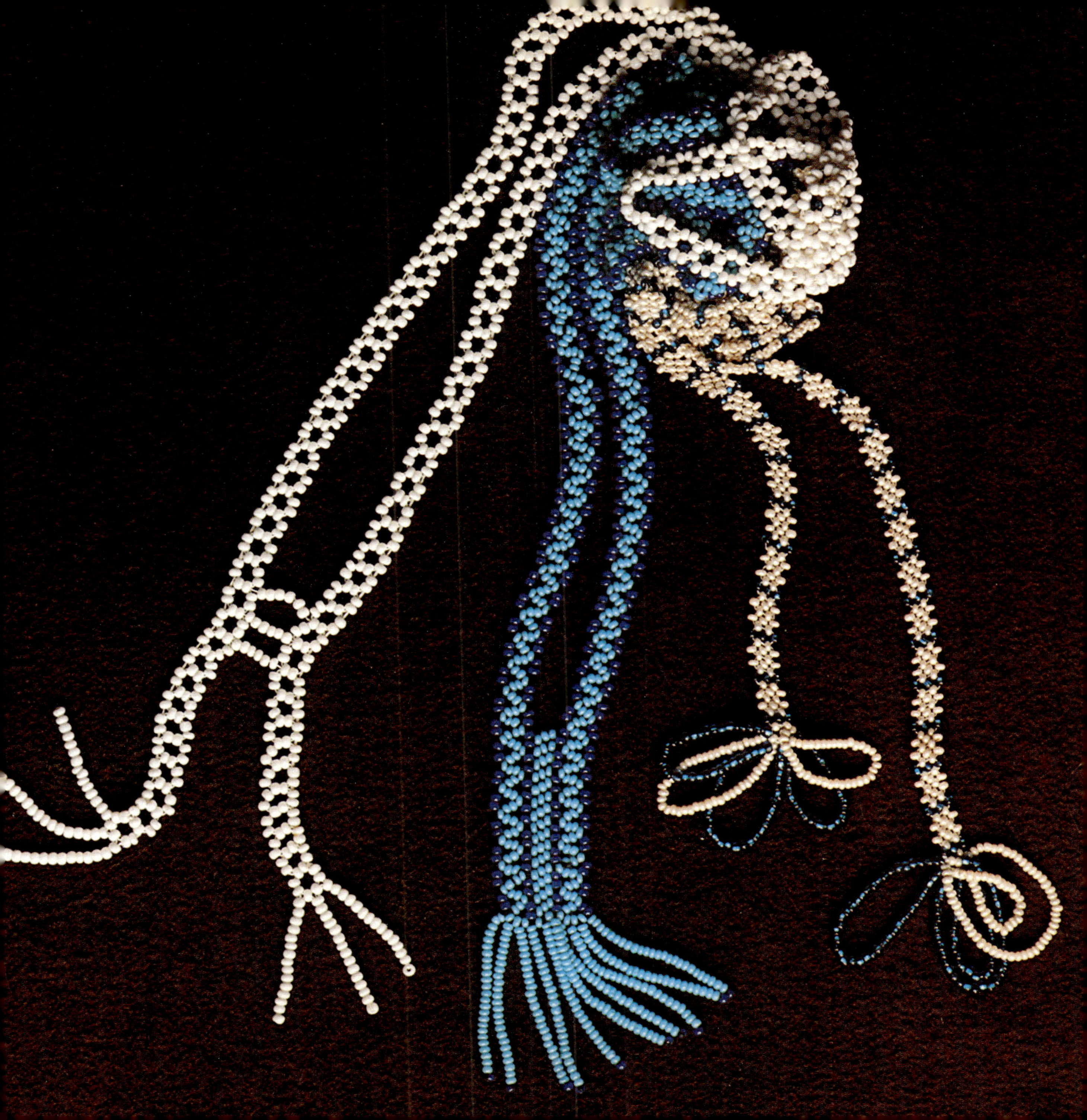

3 Thread 7m, 1c, 7m, and pass the needle through the fourth contrast bead up from the prong.
4 Thread 7m, and pass the needle through the first contrast bead along the top edge.
5 Thread 7m, 1c, 7m, and pass the needle down through the next contrast bead.
6 Repeat Stage 5 once more, and then add 7m, 1c, 1m, and form a prong as in Stage 1.

Continue working in this pattern sequence, remembering to make the prongs at the bottom edge, working up and down to form the basic necklace shape. Fasten off with the slip knot method (see Chapter 3), and attach the fastenings.

The bracelet

Key

○ = main bead (m)

— = contrast bugle bead (c)

Start

1 The top edge of the bracelet is worked first. Thread the needle with a long thread, which is then

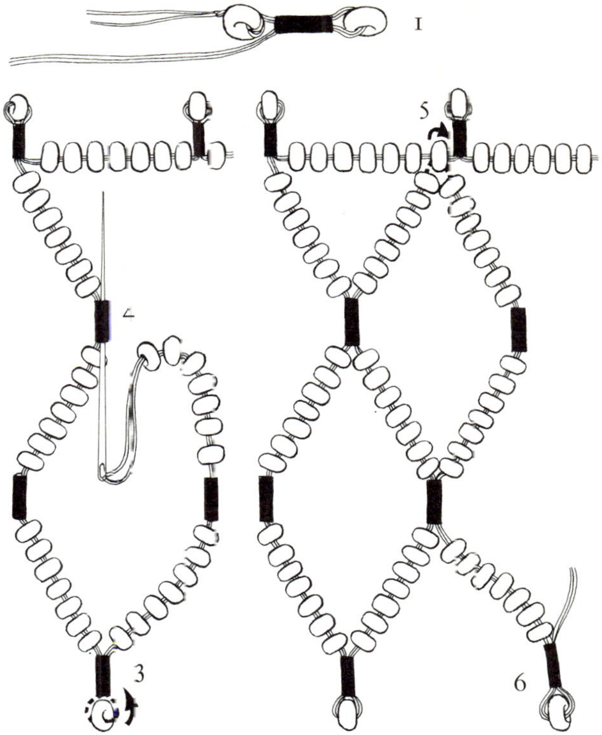

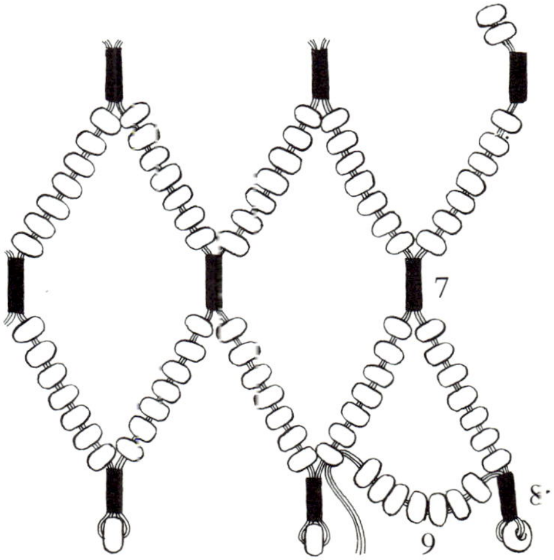

Colour plate opposite:
(*left to right*): Patterns 10, 1 and 12

doubled and waxed. Fasten thread on to one main bead and then commence pattern. Thread 1c, and 1m, and then pass the needle back through the bugle bead. Pull tightly.

2 Add 7m, 1c, 1m. Make a prong with the 1c, 1m, as in Stage 1.
Continue this until the strip fits comfortably around the wrist. Finish with a prong. The top edge of the bracelet is now complete.

3 Work down the side by adding 7m, 1c, 7m, 1c, 7m, 1c, 1m. Form the last 1c, 1m, into a prong as in Stage 1. The side of the bracelet is now complete.

4 Thread 7m, 1c, 7m, and pass the needle up through the second contrast bead from the last prong made.

5 Add 7m, and pass the needle through the seventh main bead along the top. Add 7m, 1c, 7m, and pass the needle down through the second contrast bead from the top.

6 Thread 7m, 1c, 1m, and form a prong as in Stage 1. Continue working the pattern Stages 4, 5, and 6, until the required wrist length is reached, finishing at the top edge.

7 Add 7m, 1c, 7m, and pass down through the second contrast bead.

8 Add 7m, 1c, 1m, and form another prong with these 1c, 1m, as in Stage 1.

9 To make the bottom edge, add 7c, and pass the needle through the main bead next to the prong.

10 Continue Stage 9 until all the bottom prongs have been connected. Attach the fastenings at each end.

PATTERN SIXTEEN

Collar necklace

This pattern can either be made to sit around the base of the neck or to hang fairly low at the front, as in the illustration. If the latter is required the long chains of beadwork can be added if wished. The instructions for these additions are given at the end of the pattern.

To start

Thread the needle with a very long thread. Double and wax the thread. Make a small knot 51 mm (2 in.) from the end. (When the collar necklace is completed, this excess thread will be threaded back through a few beads before cutting.) Thread one bead (main colour) and insert the needle between the two threads, between the knot and the bead. Pull tightly. Now pick up and thread enough main coloured beads for the required length. Pass the needle through the next to the last bead to prevent the thread from slipping. Pull tightly. Now you are ready to start the lacework.

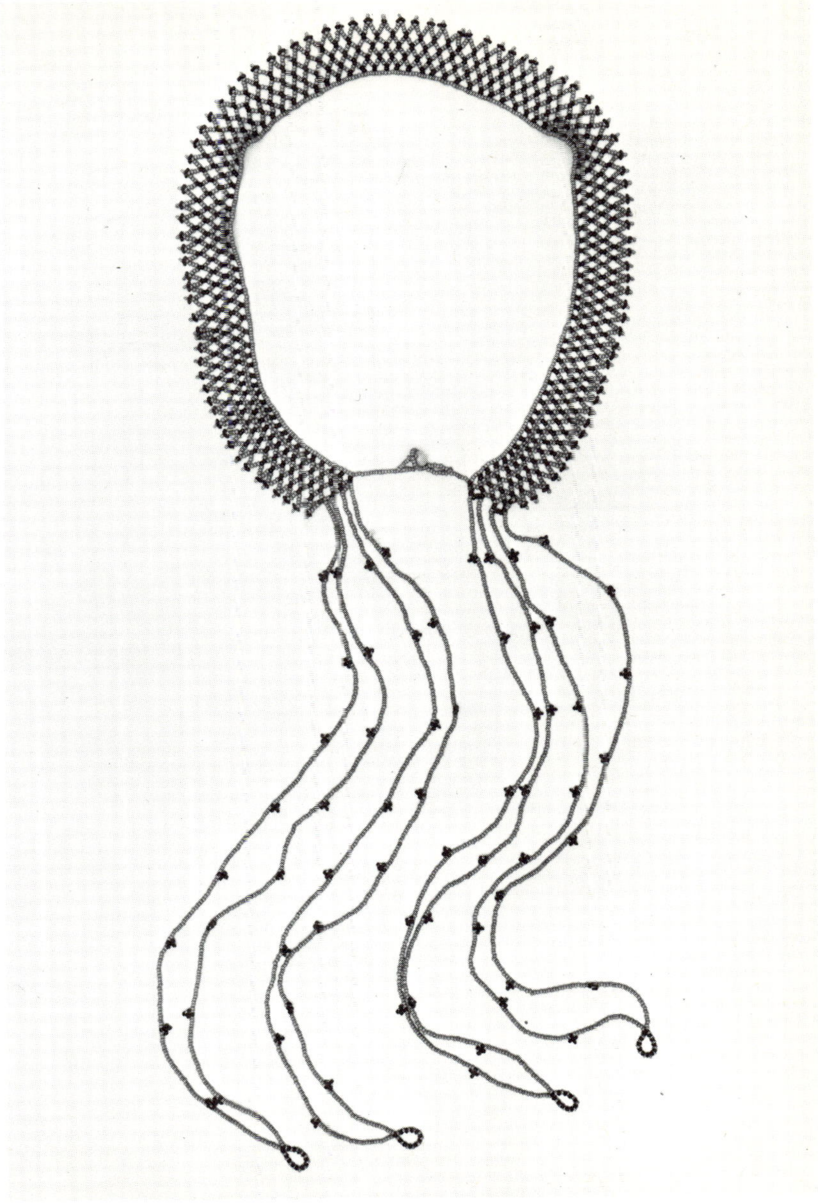

Pattern 16

Materials
2 1-oz pkts beads for main colour
1 1-oz beads for contrast colour (size optional)
2 beading needles
Drima thread
Beeswax

Key
○ = main colour (m)
● = contrast colour (c)

Pick up and thread 2c, 2m, 2c, 2m, 2c, 2m, 2c.

Pattern
1 Add 4m, 1c, 1m, 1c.
2 Pass the needle through the fourth bead from the end.
3 Add 3m, 2c, 2m, and pass the needle through 2c.
4 Add 2m, 2c, 2m, and pass the needle through 2c.
5 Pass the needle through 3m, of the top strip of beads.
6 Add 2c, 2m, and pass the needle through 2c.
7 Add 2m, 2c, 2m, and pass the needle through 2c.

Repeat Stages 1 to 7 until the collar is complete.
Add the fastenings (see Chapter 3).

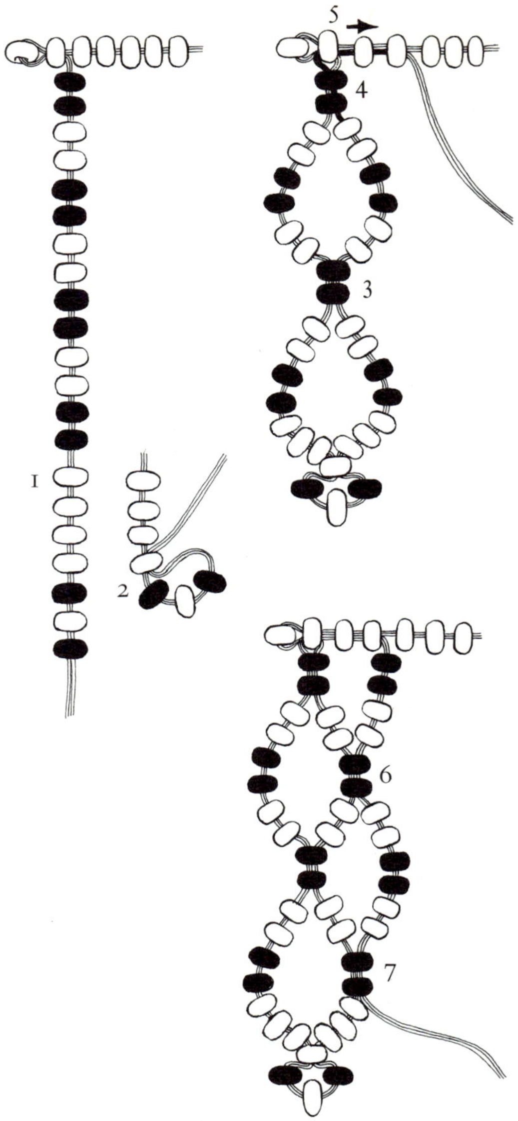

For a low hanging collar with trimmings

Thread the needle with a long thread. Double and wax it. Pass the needle through the first two contrast beads at one end of the necklace, securing it with a slip knot.

1 Add 22m, 4c.
2 Pass the needle *down* through the first contrast bead. Pull tightly.
3 Repeat 1 and 2 seven more times.
4 Add 28m, then 1c, 1m, alternately, eleven times. Pass the needle *up* through the first contrast bead. Pull tightly to form a circle.
5 Add 28m, 4c.
6 Repeat Stages 2 then 1 eight more times.

Pass the needle through 4 beads of the end of the necklace and repeat pattern Stages 1 to 6. Work the other end of the collar to match, then add fastenings (see Chapter 3).

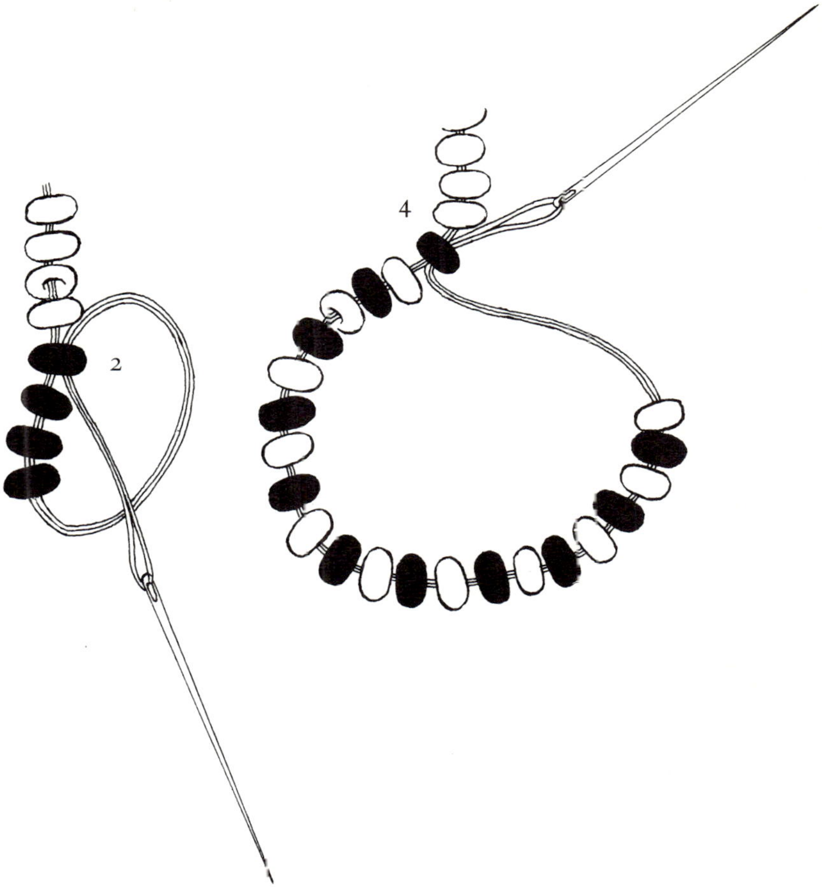

3 Techniques

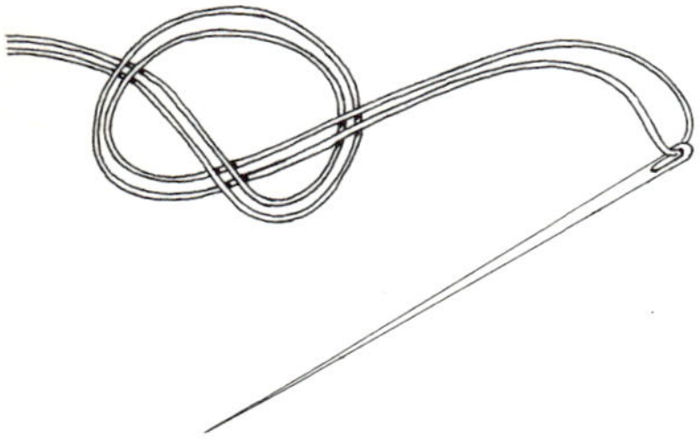

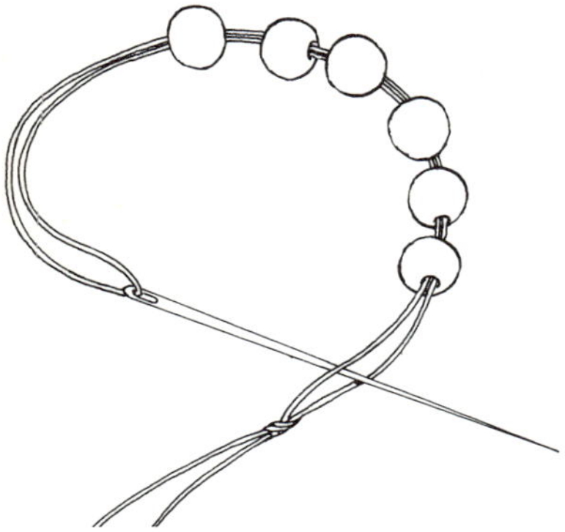

How to start each necklace
This method can be applied to any of the patterns given in Chapters 1 and 2a.
Thread the needle with a long thread. Double it and make one small knot near the end. Run the thread twice through beeswax to strengthen the thread and to prevent tangling.
Thread the required number of beads (usually six), and pass the needle between the two threads in the space between the knot and the first bead.
Pull tightly and a circle is formed.

Renewing thread
Thread the needle with long double thread (no knot) and run it through beeswax.
Insert the needle into a bead in the second or third flower down. Leaving a short 'tail', do one slip knot (see below). Pass the needle through two more beads before doing another slip knot. Continue in this way until the thread reaches the first flower and then, omitting slip knots, pass the needle through the remaining beads until it comes out of the same bead as the previous thread.
Continue the necklace with the new thread.
When you have completed approximately 50 mm (2 in.) pick up the first needle and anchor the thread by working two or three slip knots in the first two flowers above the thread. Run the needle through two more beads and cut the thread (fig. 3).

Slip knots
Dressmakers know this as a button-hole stitch. A new thread is always attached by this method. *Never* have a knot at the end.

A slip knot is made by forming a complete circle with the thread and then inserting the needle into the centre of this circle, scooping all the threads inside the circle, between the bead out of which you have just come and the bead into which you are just going. Pull the thread tightly.

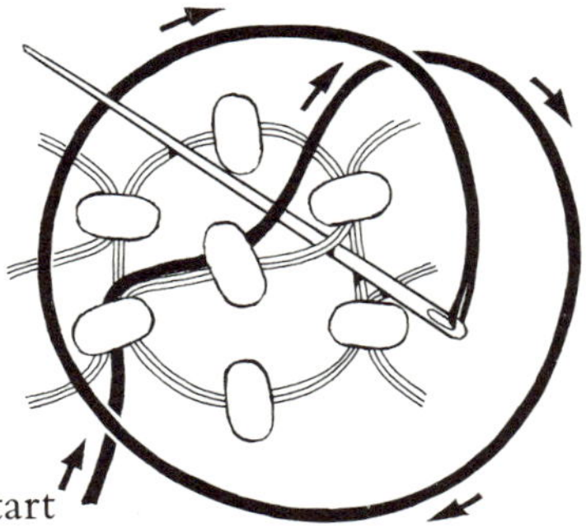

The slip knot

To make a circular necklace
Work the desired length and then work the thread through the opposite end, doing a series of slip knots to anchor the thread. Cut.

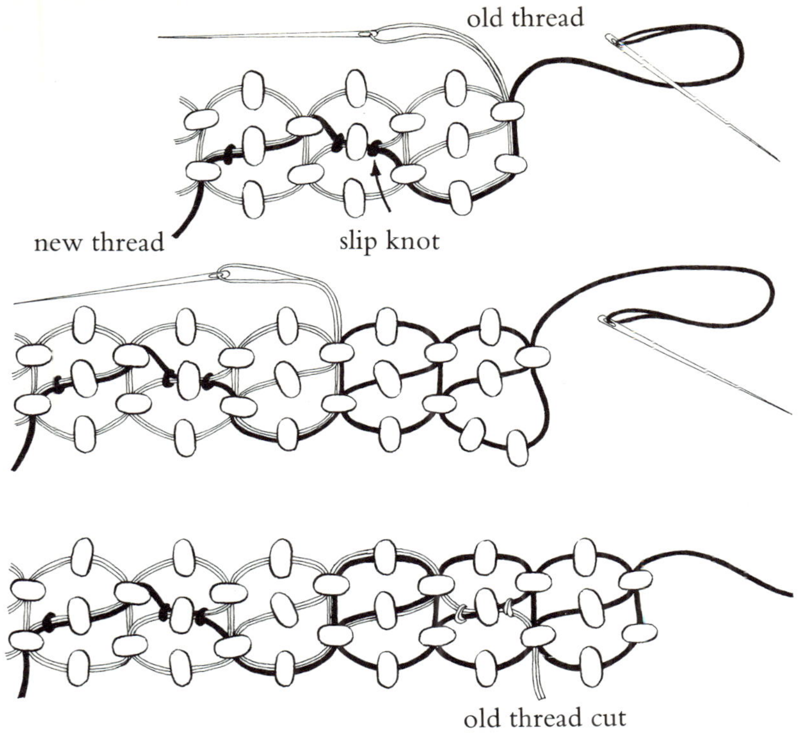

(*above*): Renewing thread

(*below*): Joining a circular necklace

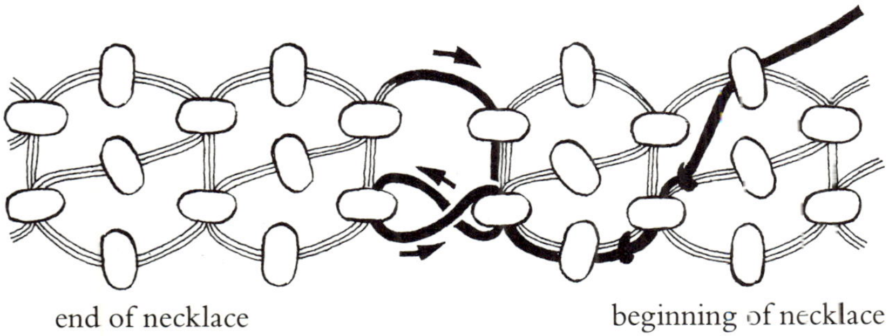

To join two ends together

Key
○ = beads of necklace (n)
● = beads for joining (b)

1 Using the slip knot method fasten the end of a long, double, waxed thread into the bottom of one end of the necklace.
2 Thread 2b, and pass the needle through the outside bead of the first flower at the opposite end of the necklace.
3 Thread 1b, and pass the needle through bead A below, and up through bead n, of the opposite flower. Pull tightly.
4 Thread 2b, and pass through bead B below, and up through bead n, of the second flower.

Repeat Stages 3 and 4 until the desired length is achieved. (This is usually 38–51 mm ($1\frac{1}{2}$–2 in.)

Finish
Work two or three slip knots into one side of the necklace. Cut the thread.

1
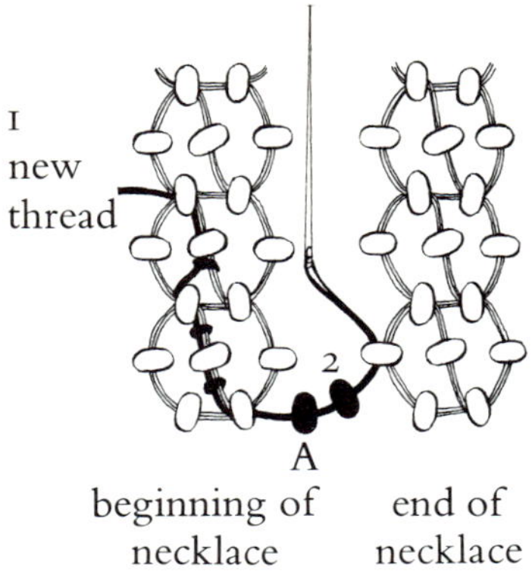

3
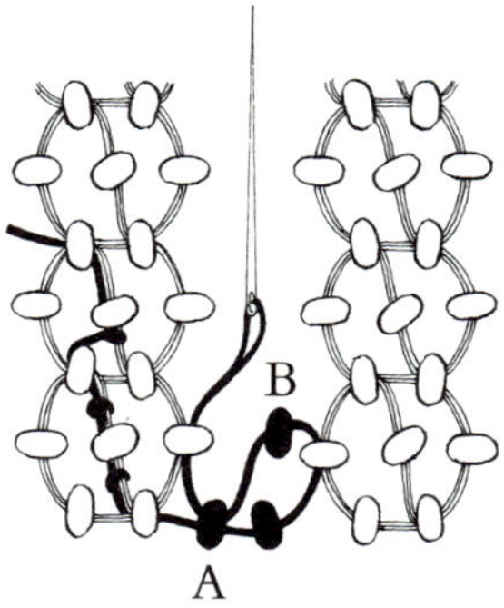

4
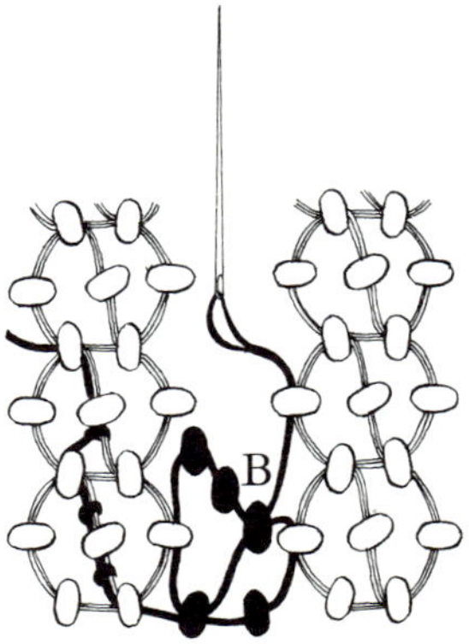

Joining necklace ends—slip knot method

Fringes
Key
● = main colour (m)
○ = contrast colour (c)

Run a long, double thread through beeswax (*no knot*). Starting at one end of the necklace, work two or three slip knots through the beads to anchor the thread and bring the needle out through the first bead at the end.

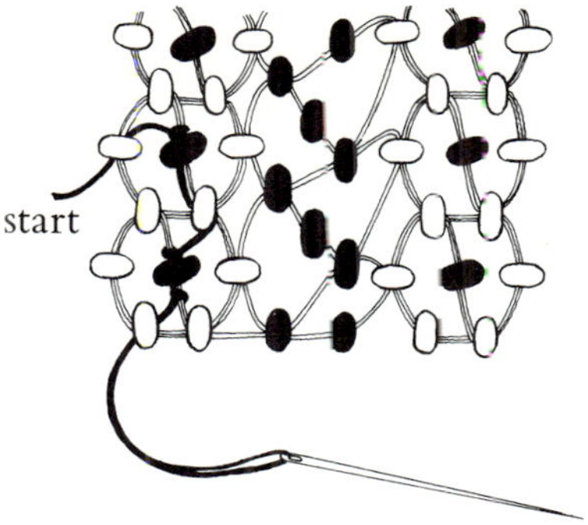

Fringe
★Thread 10m (the number varies according to the length of the fringe) and 3c. Work the needle back through to the first c threaded through all beads m.★
Pass the needle through the next bead, 2, and repeat from ★ to ★. Repeat with beads 3, 4, 5, and 6, or until all the bottom beads are fringed.
Finish off by doing two or three slip knots into the necklace, to anchor the thread.

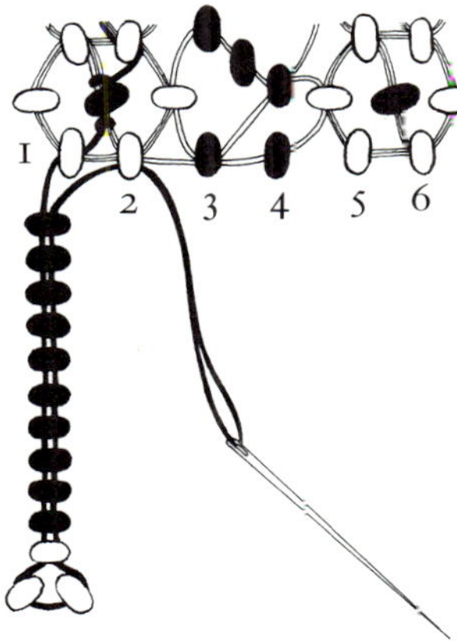

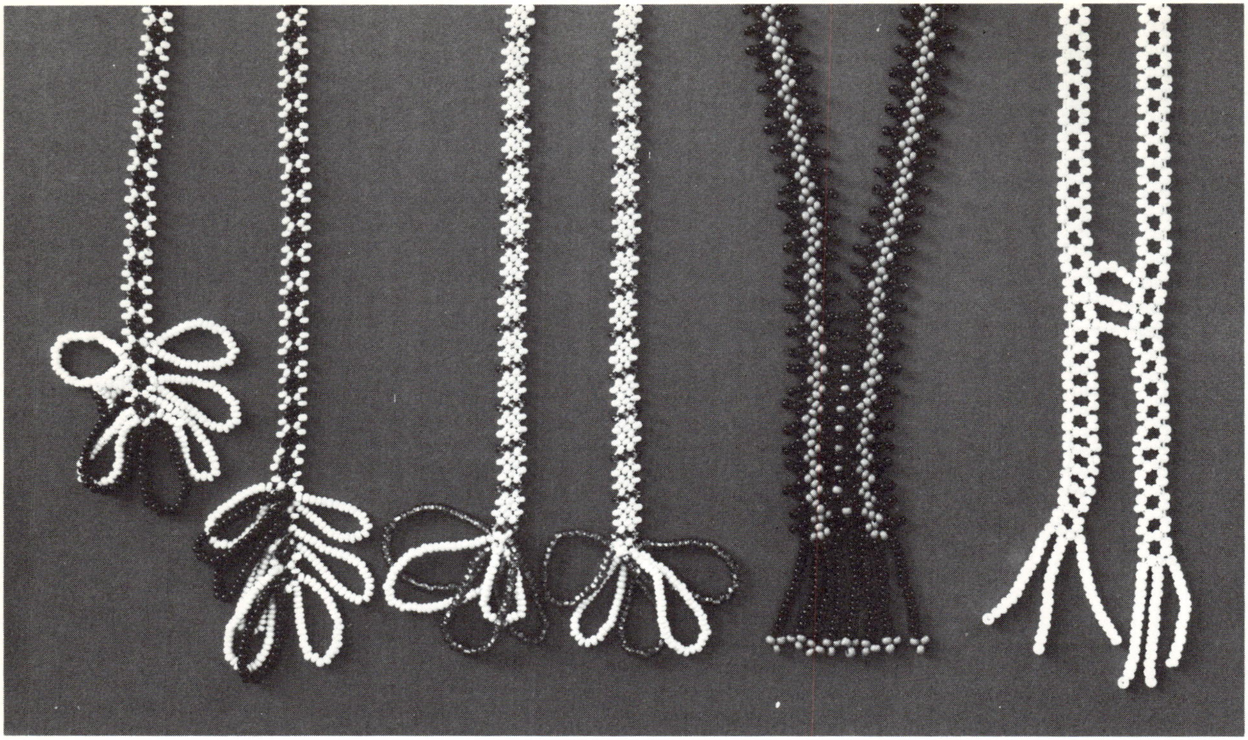

fringes

4 Wooden beads

PATTERN SEVENTEEN This pattern is for making a choker or a bracelet.

Key

○ = small outside beads (s)

● = large centre beads (c)

Materials

For a 318 mm ($12\frac{1}{2}$ in.) choker:

68 8 mm ($\frac{3}{8}$ in.) round wooden beads

16 12 mm ($\frac{1}{2}$ in.) wooden beads for contrast

Buttonhole twist or thin cord

Take a long piece of thin cord. Double the cord and pin the centre onto a cushion or a piece of polystyrene. Dip the two ends of the cord separately into nail polish to make stiff ends.

Pattern

1 Thread 2s beads onto each thread.

2 Take the right-hand cord and thread one c bead. Pass the left-hand cord through this same bead in the opposite direction.

3 Repeat Stages 1 and 2 of the pattern for the desired length.

Fasten both cords back into the beadwork using slip knots, and attach the fastenings, both methods described in Chapter 3.

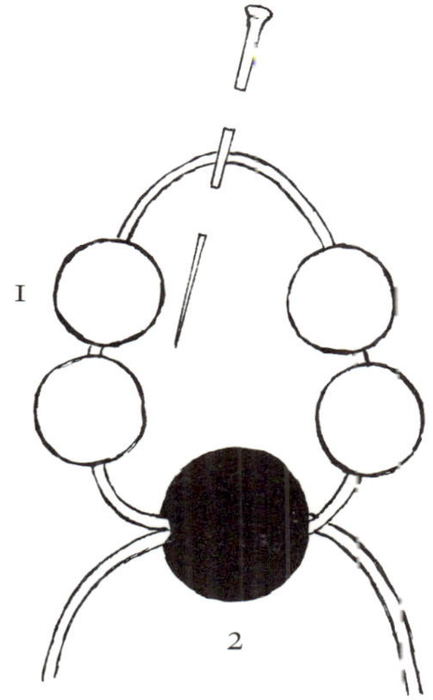

PATTERN EIGHTEEN A design for a pendant necklace.

Materials
72 8 mm ($\frac{3}{8}$ in.) round wooden beads
Buttonhole twist, or thin cord
1 large needle.

Start

a Thread the needle with a long cord and make a knot 76 mm (3 in.) from the end.
b Thread 1 bead and pass the needle through the knot. Pull tightly to secure the bead.
c Thread 21 beads and pass the needle through the first bead to form a circle.
d Pass the needle through the next four beads (i.e. beads 2, 3, 4 and 5), and thread 12 beads. Pass the needle through beads 11, 12, and 13.
e Thread 12 beads and pass the needle through up bead 19.
f Pass the needle round through all the beads and down through beads a, b, and c, as illustrated: (opposite).
g Thread 9 beads and pass the needle up through beads d, e, and f.
h Pass the needle through the beads again bringing it down through beads a, b, and c.
i Thread 17 beads and pass the needle up through beads d, e, and f.

The pendant is now complete. Fasten the thread off by using the slip knot method described in Chapter 3. Attach the pendant to a chain, or leather thong.

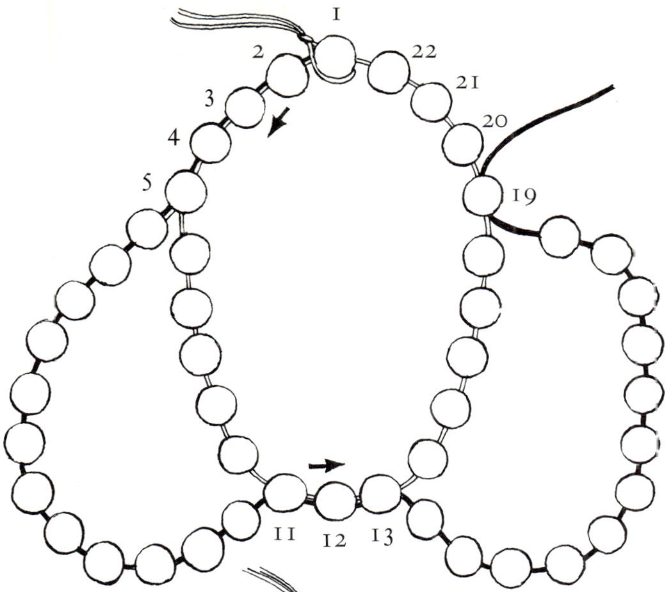
1
2
3
4
5
22
21
20
19
11
12
13

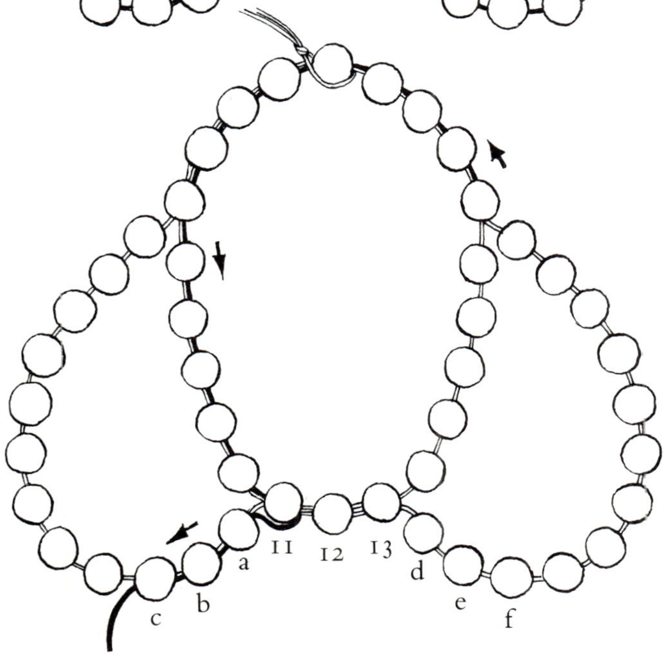
11
12
13
a
b
c
d
e
f

PATTERN NINETEEN A flower design, suitable for a choker, bracelet, or belt.

Key

○ = gold background beads (g)
● = purple flower beads (pr)
⊗ = pink flower beads (pk)

Materials

200 8 mm ($\frac{3}{8}$ in.) beads
84 8 mm ($\frac{3}{8}$ in.) beads
14 8 mm ($\frac{3}{8}$ in.) beads
(To make a choker 356 mm (14 in.) long)
Buttonhole twist
1 needle

Start

1 Thread the needle and make a knot 76 mm (3 in.) from the end. Thread 1g, insert the needle through the knot, and pull tightly to secure the bead.
2 Thread 2g and turn the work over (bottom to top).
3 Thread 1g and insert the needle back through the last g bead.
4 Thread 1g and insert the needle through the first bead strung. Turn the work over.
5 Thread 1pr and insert the needle through the side g bead.
6 Thread 1g and insert the needle through the top g bead.

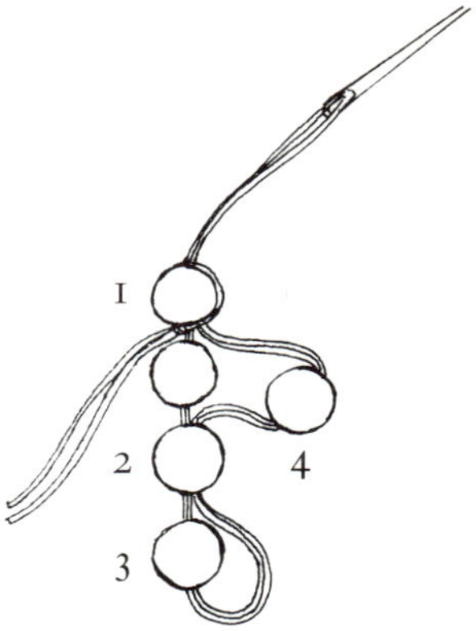

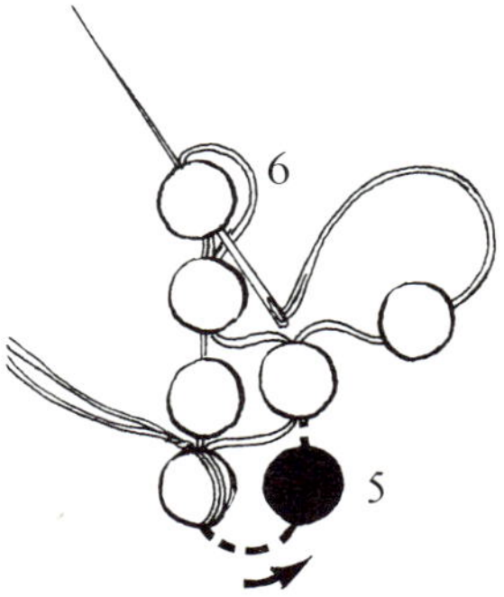

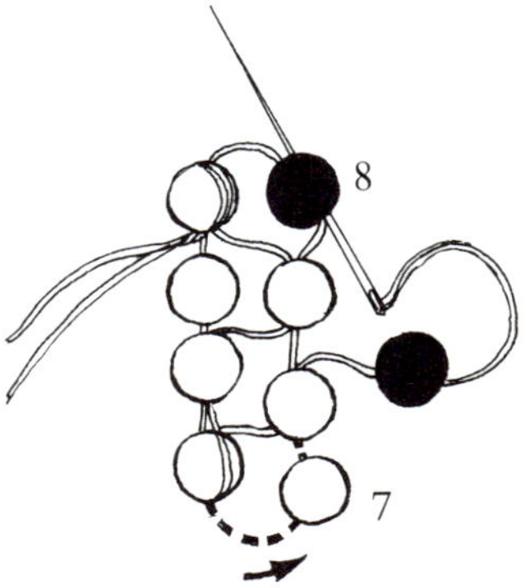

7 Turn the work over. Thread 1g and insert the needle through the side g bead.
8 Thread 1pr and insert the needle through the pr bead.
9 Turn the work over. Thread 2pr and 1pk, and insert the needle through the top pr bead.
10 Thread 1g and insert the needle through the top g bead. Turn the work over. Thread 1g and insert the needle through the side g bead.
11 Thread 1pr and insert the needle through the pk bead. Turn the work over.
12 Thread 1 pr and insert the needle through the pr bead above.
13 Pass the needle through all pr beads and back to the starting point. Pull the thread tightly. Thread 1g and insert the needle through the g bead at the top. This completes one flower.

Pattern

1 Turn the work over and begin the second flower by threading 1 pr and insert the needle through the g bead above.
2 Thread 1g and insert the needle through the second

pr bead above. Turn the work over.

3 Thread 1g and insert the needle through the g bead above.

4 Thread 1pr and insert the needle through the pr bead above. Turn the work over.

5 Thread 2pr 1pk and insert the needle through the pr bead above.

6 Thread 1g and insert the needle through the top g bead. Turn the work over.

7 Thread 1g and insert the needle through the g bead above.

8 Thread 1pr and insert the needle through the pk bead above. Turn the work over.

9 Thread 1pr and insert the needle through the pr bead above.

10 Pass the needle through all the pr beads and back to the starting point. Pull tightly.

11 Thread 1g and insert the needle through the top g bead.

The second flower is now complete. Repeat Stages 1 to 11 of the pattern for the desired length.
Attach the fastenings, as described in Chapter 3.

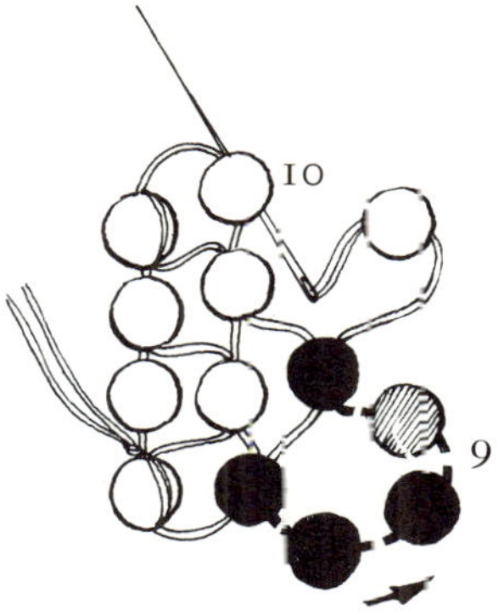

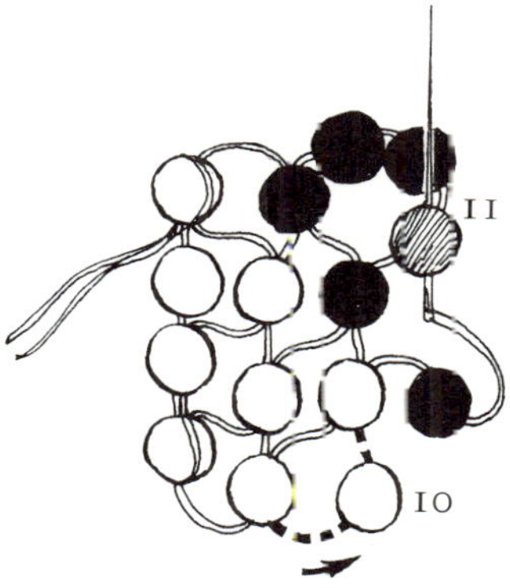

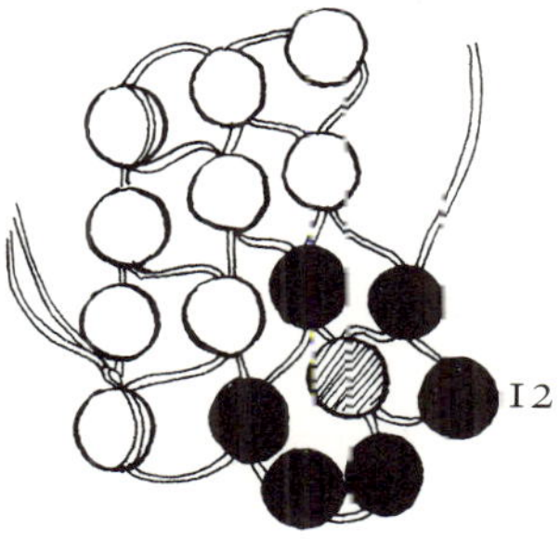

PATTERN TWENTY A ladder belt design.

Equipment
2 large-eyed needles
A piece of cardboard, 140 mm ($5\frac{1}{2}$ in.) wide

Materials
Crochet cord to match beads chosen
29 oval brown wooden beads, 18 × 8 mm ($\frac{3}{4}$ in. × $\frac{3}{8}$ in.)
280 aqua round beads, 8 mm ($\frac{3}{8}$ in.)

Key
○ = outside beads (b)
● = oval or large, round beads (r)

Directions
Start with two very long strands of crochet cord. Knot the two ends together, leaving 127 mm (5 in.) long ends. Thread each remaining end separately through 2 needles. Insert one needle through one r bead, and insert the other needle through the other end of the same bead.
Thread 5b beads onto each cord. Then insert one needle through another r bead. Insert the other needle through the other end of the same bead. Repeat this operation 27 more times, ending with an r bead. Knot the cords together leaving a long end of about 127 mm (5 in.).

To make the tassel
Wrap the cord, about 80 times around a piece of cardboard. Using the ends of the cord from one end of the ladder belt, tie the strands at one end of the cardboard, securing the strands at the same time. Knot tightly. Cut through the strands at the opposite ends of the card. Bring the cut ends together. Tightly wrap the strands twice, about 25 mm (1 in.) below the knotted end, with a separate strand of cord. Knot securely. Trim the cut ends evenly.
Make a second tassel for the other end of the belt.

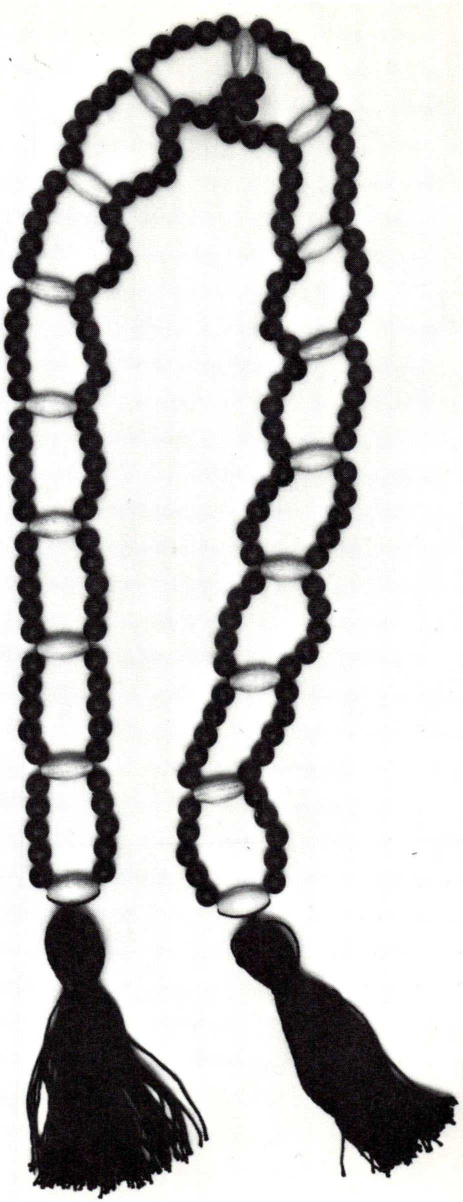

Pattern 20

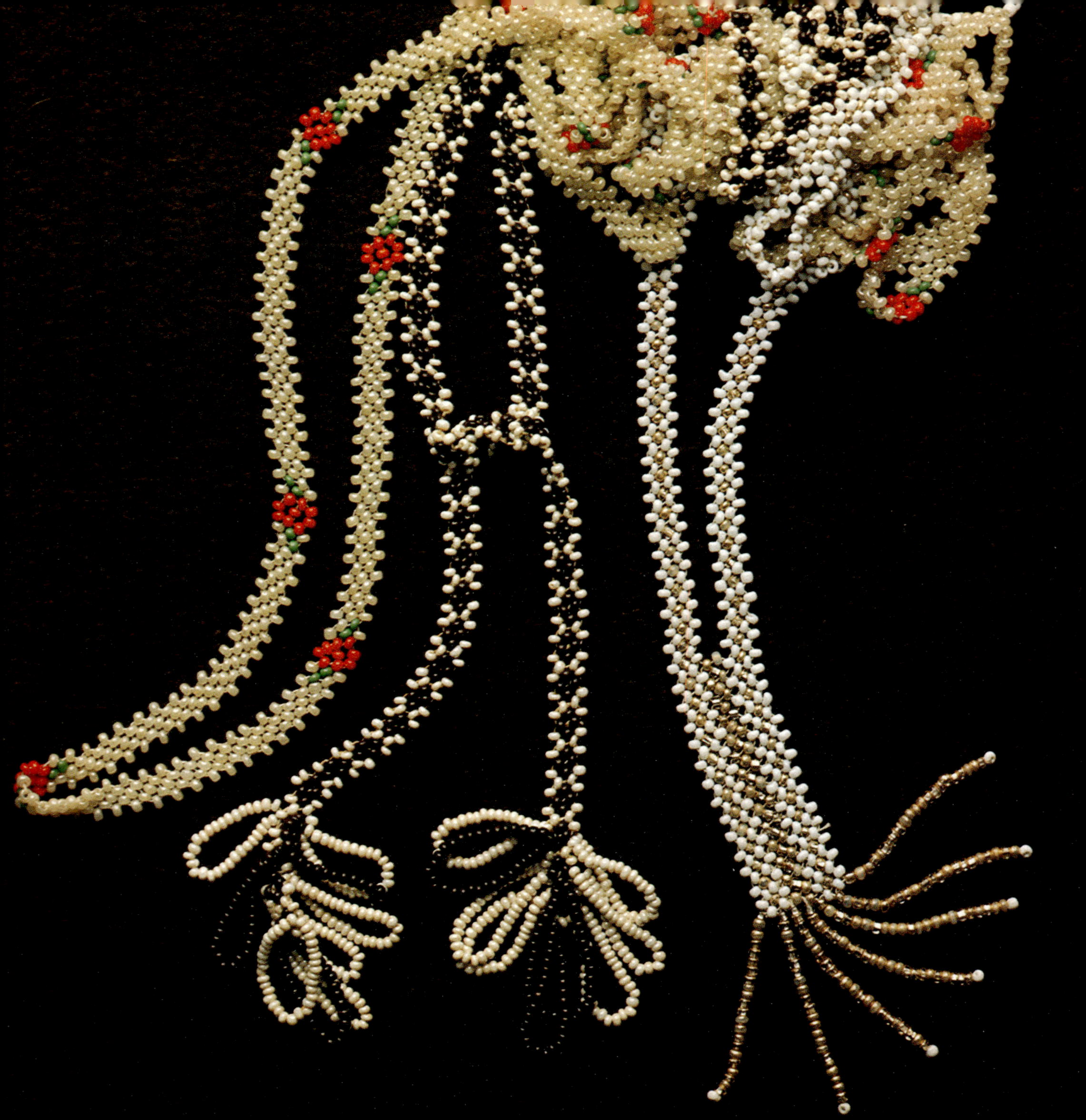

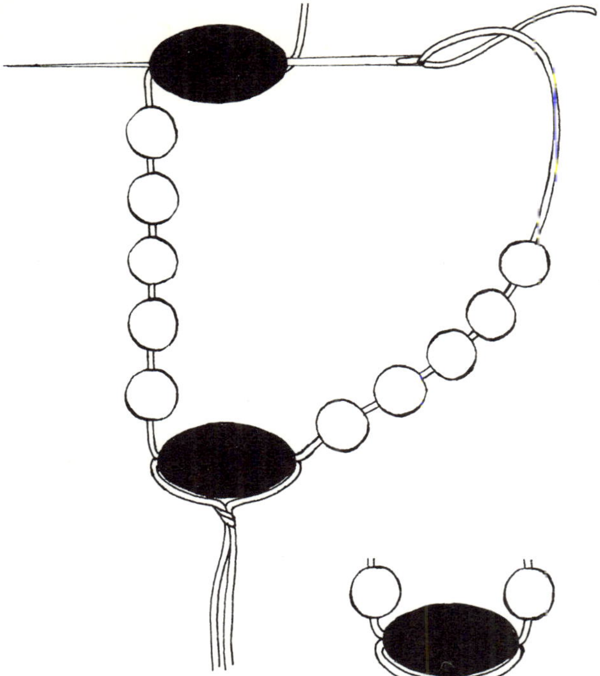

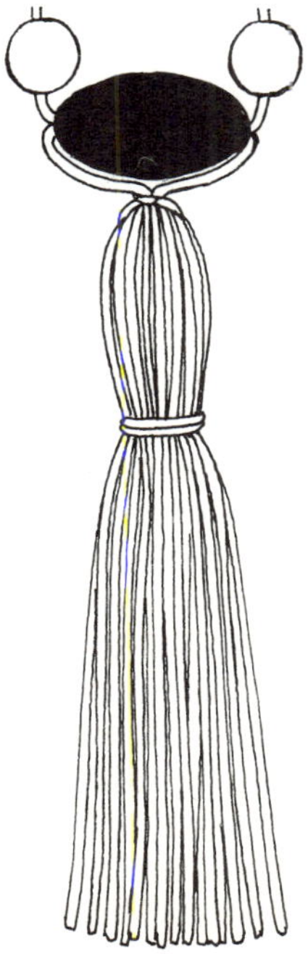

Colour plate opposite:
(*left to right*) Patterns 6, 9 and 12

PATTERN TWENTY-ONE

A daisy chain suitable for a necklace, bracelet, belt, or trim.

Materials

Two flowers with a connecting link measures 76 mm (3 in.) and requires:

16 8 mm ($\frac{3}{8}$ in.) round wooden beads for flowers

2 12 mm ($\frac{1}{2}$ in.) round beads of contrasting colour for centres

5 8 mm ($\frac{3}{8}$ in.) round wooden beads of third colour for link

2 large-eyed needles

Button twist or thin cord

Key

○ = petal (p) ⊗ = centre (c)

● = link beads connecting the flowers (b)

Pattern

1 Take a long cord and thread a needle onto each end. Draw one p bead into the centre of the cord.

The following operation is made easier if the beginning of the necklace is pinned onto a cushion.

2 Thread seven p on to the left needle. Pass the needle through the right-hand side of the first bead. Pull tightly to form a circle.

3 Thread 1c onto the left-hand needle and pass the right-hand needle through the opposite end of the c bead.

4 Pass the left-hand needle through the middle p bead on the opposite side of the flower and pass the right-hand needle through the same bead but in the opposite direction. Pull tightly.

5 Thread 1b onto each needle.

6 Thread 1b onto the left-hand needle and pass the right-hand needle through the same b bead, but in the opposite direction.

7 Now thread one b onto each needle.

8 For the second flower, thread one p onto the left-hand needle and pass the right-hand needle through this same bead p in the opposite direction.

9 Now continue working pattern Stages 2 to 8 for the desired length.

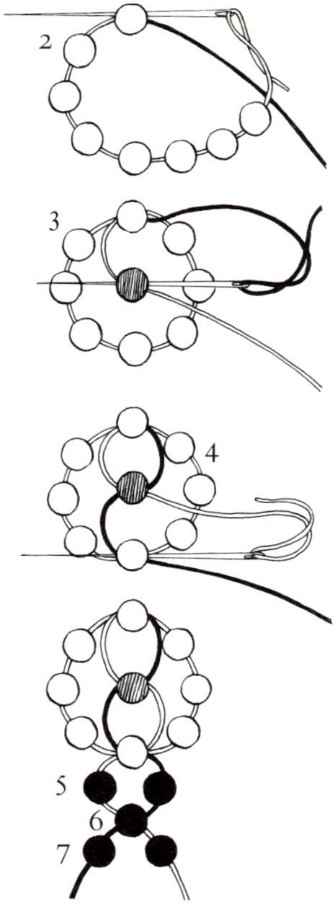

PATTERN TWENTY-TWO

A design for deep edging, coming to a point which could be used as a wall hanging.

Materials

To make an edge 152 mm (6 in.) wide:

63 8 mm ($\frac{3}{8}$ in.) round wooden beads for main colour

9 8 mm ($\frac{3}{8}$ in.) round wooden beads for contrast

Thin cord

Large-eyed needle

Key

○ = main beads (m)

● = contrast beads (c)

Start

1 Fasten the thread into one end of the edge of the fabric. Thread 3m, 1c, 3m, and catch the thread in the fabric 38 mm ($1\frac{1}{2}$ in.) further along the edge.
Repeat this all along the edge.

2 To make the second and successive rows, bring the needle back through the last 3m, 1c threaded.
Thread 3m, 1c, 3m and pass the needle through c bead of the next loop.

3 The bottom may be finished with a wide loop. Fasten the thread off with slip knots (see Chapter 3).

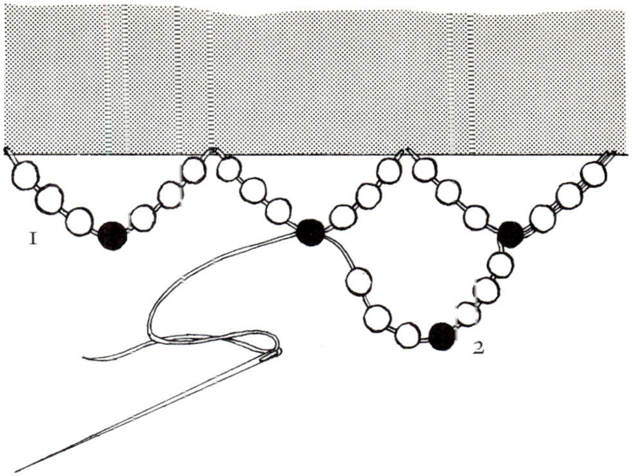

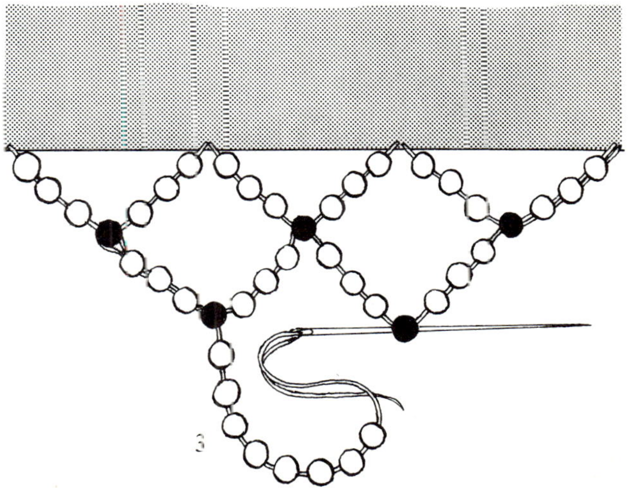

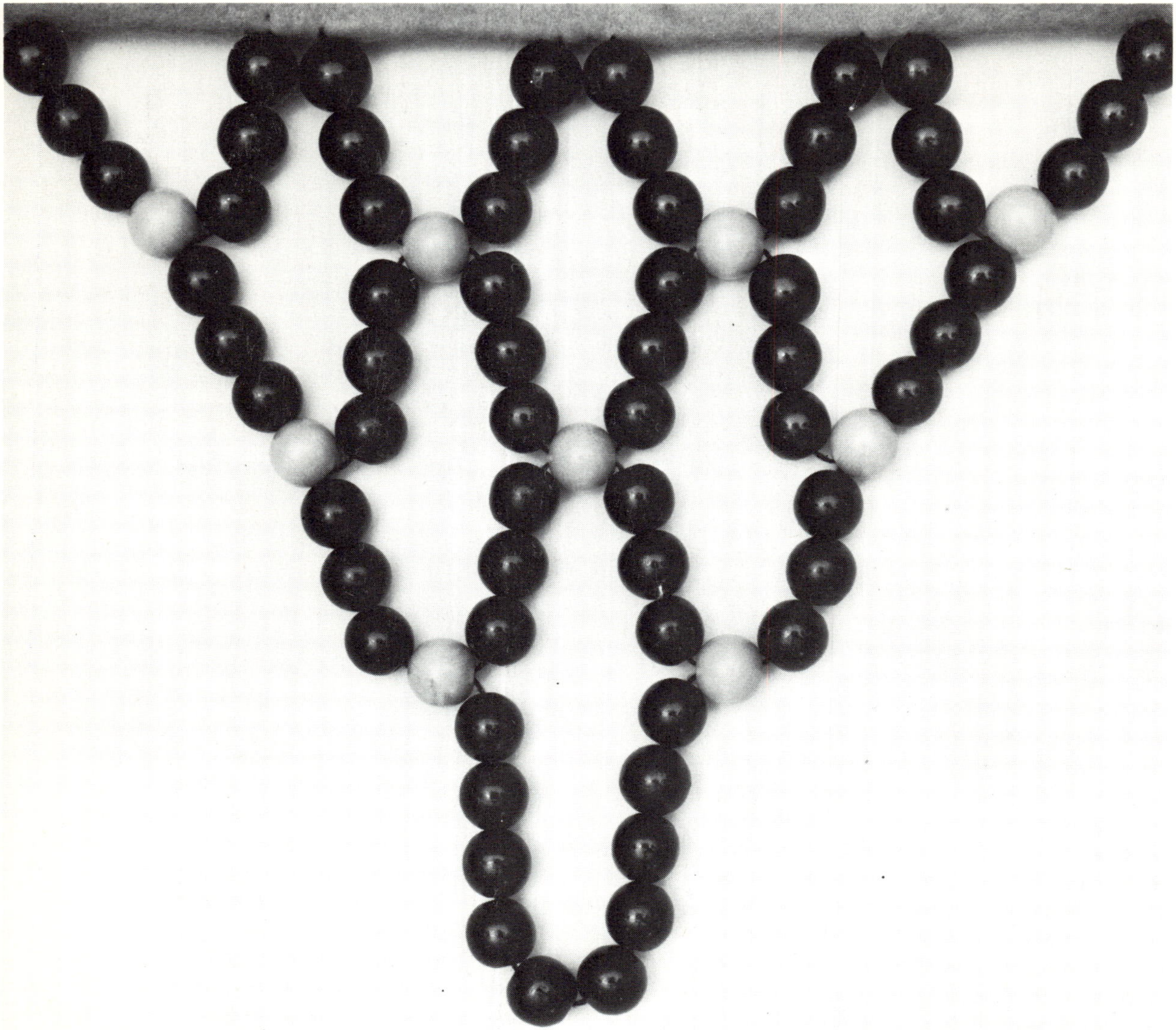

Pattern 22

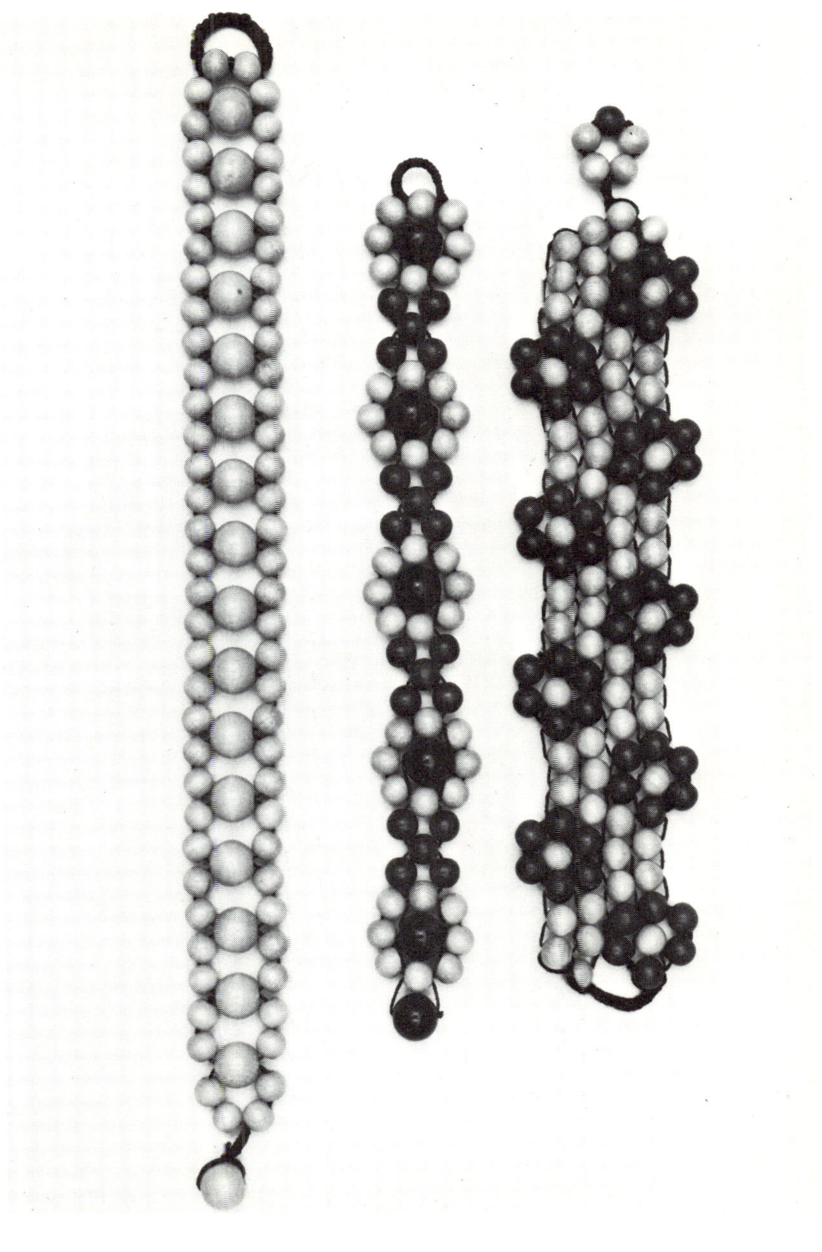

(*left to right*): Patterns 17, 21 and 19

Part 2 Loom beadwork

5 The loom

Very little equipment is needed for bead weaving. To produce a flat ribbon of closely-woven beadwork, a bead loom is essential. The beadloom illustrated is inexpensive, indestructible, and the double rollers permit any length of work to be made. (For suppliers, see page 94.)

It is possible to construct a loom from a wooden box with tacks hammered into it (fig. a). Even a cardboard box with notches cut into the edges can be used as a loom, but the threads must be stretched very tightly before work is begun, and only very small pieces of beadweaving can be worked by this method.

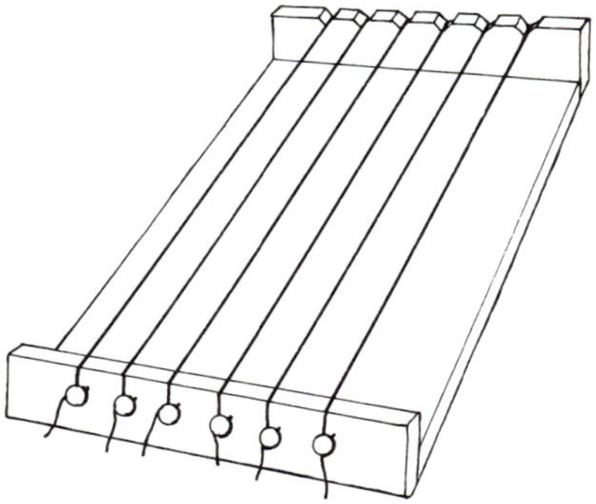

Key

☒ = red (r)
○ = blue (b)
• = black (bk)
☐ = background white (w)

All the loom patterns in Chapter 7 are worked from a graph. Many people, however, find reading from a graph tiresome. The 'knitting pattern' method which follows each graph design eliminates this drawback, and many people find it a speedier way of following a design. The following graph design would read:

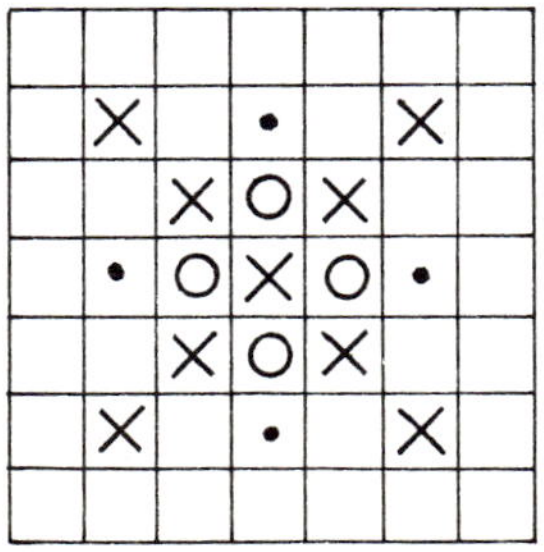

1 7w
2 1w 1r 1w 1bk 1w 1r 1w
3 2w 1r 1b 1r 2w
4 1w 1bk 1b 1r 1b 1bk 1w
5 2w 1r 1b 1r 2w
6 1w 1r 1w 1bk 1w 1r 1w

Threading the loom

Choose the design, decide on the length of the finished work, and then add 355 mm (14 in.). This is the length which is needed for each warp thread. One more warp thread than the number of beads in the width of the design is also required. Therefore, if the design is eight beads wide, nine threads are used.

To start

1 Tie a knot at each end of the bundle of threads.
2 Split the threads roughly into halves and pass one knot over the rivet on one roller.
3 Loosen the wing-nut and roll on the thread until the other knot can be placed over the rivet on the other roller.
4 Using a beading needle, lift the threads into place in the SPRING SEPARATOR in such a way that each thread passes

through one 'notch'. There must not be any empty 'notches' between each thread (unless large beads are used).

5 The threads should lie parallel and can be tightened, using one of the rollers. Your loom is now ready for use.

Threading the beads

1 Thread the needle with a long, double thread and draw this thread through the beeswax.

2 Place your beads in a small, oblong container, e.g. a tobacco tin, and use a 'scooping' motion to thread the beads on to the needle. (Fig. a.)

a

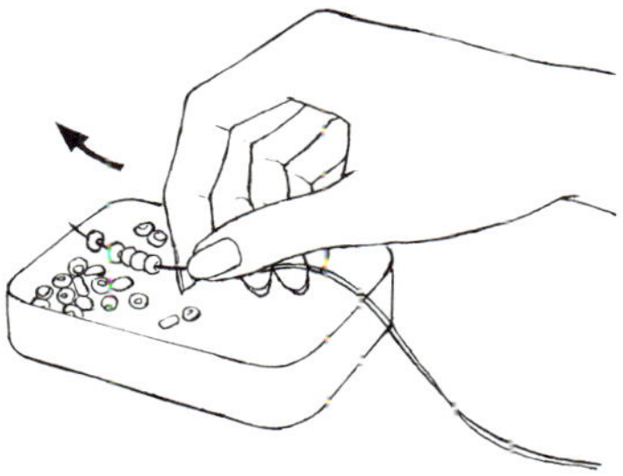

Threading the beads onto the loom

1 Tie the loose ends of the thread onto the left-hand side warp thread where it is intended to start the bead-work. This is usually fairly close to one of the rollers.

2 Pass the needle and thread underneath the warp threads. (Fig. b.)

3 Pick up the necessary beads for the first line and slide them along the thread until they are underneath the spaces between the warp threads of the loom.

4 With a finger below the beads, push the beads through the spaces between the warp threads and push the needle once again through the beads in the opposite direction and above the warp threads. (Fig. c.)

This will secure the beads in place on the loom.

Pull the thread tight and straighten them in a row.

All the other rows are secured in the same way, but do not tie a knot at the beginning of each row.

b

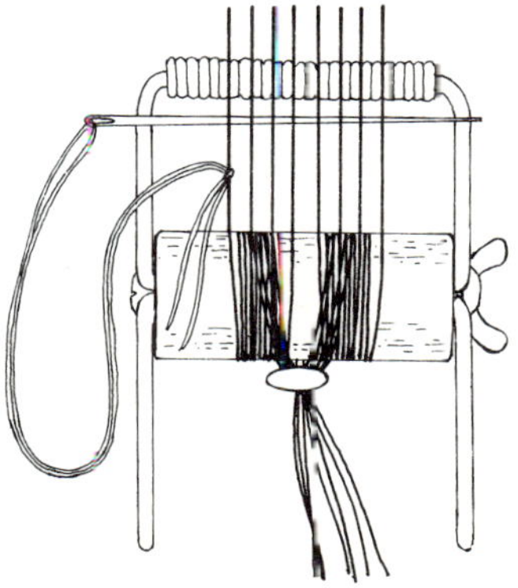

c

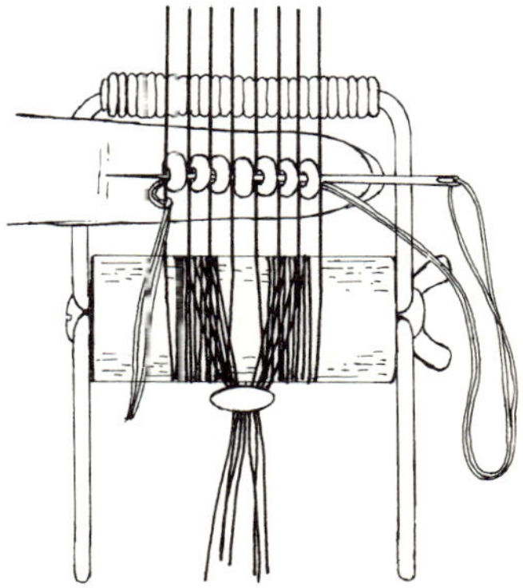

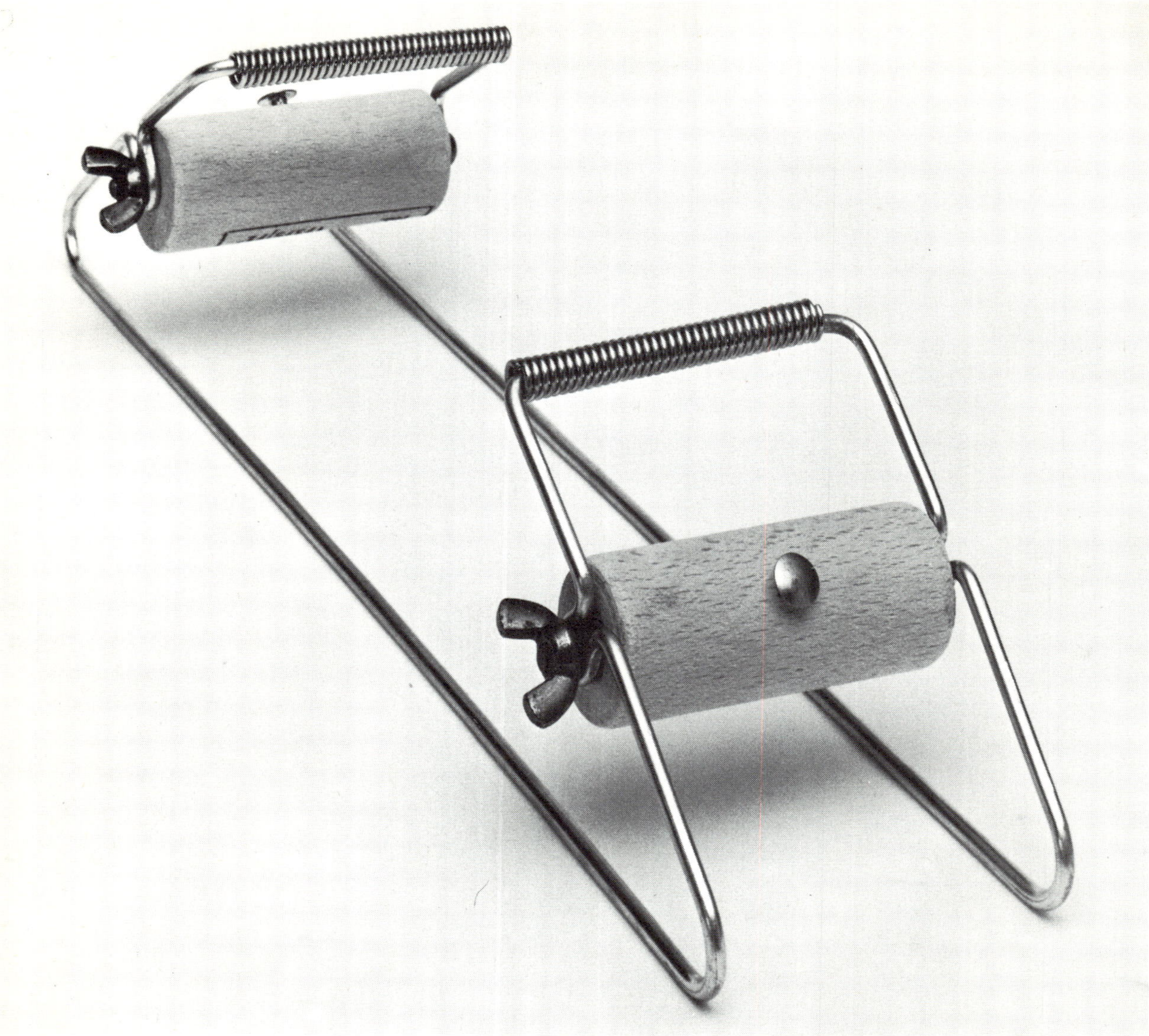

The beadworking loom

6 Beginnings and endings

Beginning a pointed fringed necklace

Roll 200 mm (8 in.) of thread on to the bottom roller before commencing (this thread will later be used for fringing). Knot the thread to one of the centre threads and start with a single bead in the centre. Add two beads to each succeeding row according to the pattern. The weaving thread will show up quite markedly along one side of the point, but this will be well hidden when the fringe is added.

Beginning a fringed necklace with a square bottom

Roll sufficient thread on to the bottom roller for fringing, and then tie the weaving thread to the first warp thread. Leave a long tail. (When the beadwork is finished, thread this tail on to the needle and pass through a few beads before cutting). Start weaving as described in Chapter 5.

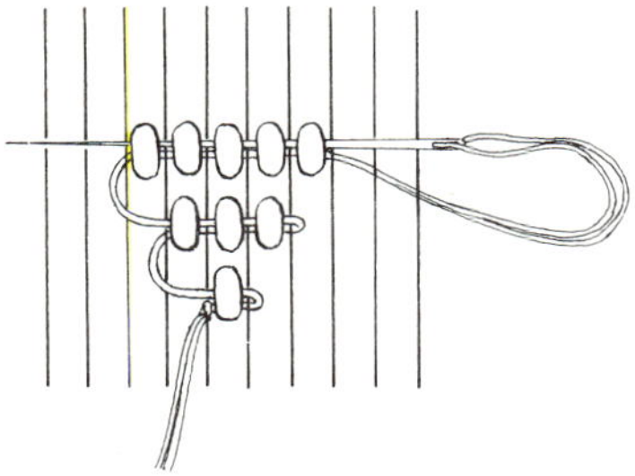

The weaving is not limited in length to the distance between the two separators, but can be continuously rolled on to one of the rollers as the length of work increases.

When rolling the completed part of the weaving over the rivet on the roller, a small pad of paper placed between the work and the rivet head will help to keep the weaving flat.

The warp threads need not be placed in every notch of the separator. For example, if large wooden beads are being woven the warp threads are placed in every fourth or fifth notch according to the diameter of the respective beads.

Beginning a belt choker or bracelet

Thread the needle with a long thread, double, and wax it. Tie the weaving thread to the first warp thread. Work 10 rows without beads in darning stitch to form a selvedge, finishing on the left. This will later be glued underneath the beadwork to form a neat edge. Now start beadweaving as described in Chapter 5.

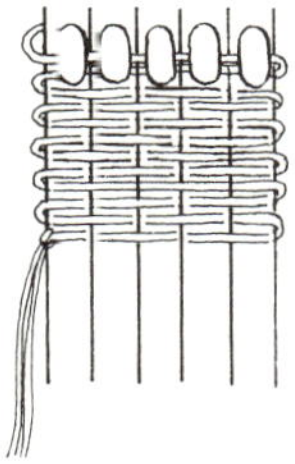

(*above left*): Beginning a pointed fringed necklace
(*above*): Beginning a belt, choker, or bracelet

To renew thread

To conceal the end of the old thread
Pass the needle through the first three beads of the next but last row. Knot the thread at x using the slip-knot method (see Chapter 3). Pass the needle through the remaining beads of the same row. Cut the thread.

Adding a new piece of weaving thread
Thread the needle with a long double thread and wax it. Pass the needle through several beads of the last row and make a slip knot at point y (see Chapter 3). Pass the needle through the remaining beads and continue with the work.

To divide the beadwork as in a necklace
When the division point is reached in making a necklace, move half the warp threads two notches to one side.
Continue working on the left-hand threads, ignoring the right-hand half of the warp threads.
When the left-hand side is finished, fasten the thread into the next but last row as described above.
Roll the beadwork back to the beginning of the division. Take a needle with a long thread—double and wax it. Tie it to the first of the right-hand warp threads.
Leave a long tail. When the necklace is completed, thread this tail through a few beads before cutting.
When both sides have been completed, remove the necklace from the loom and finish off as described below.

When the necklace narrows
When the pattern requires you to reduce the number of beads per row, the first and last warp threads are not required. Ignore these until the work is completed and then work each warp thread into the beadwork, securing it with a slip knot as in Chapter 3.

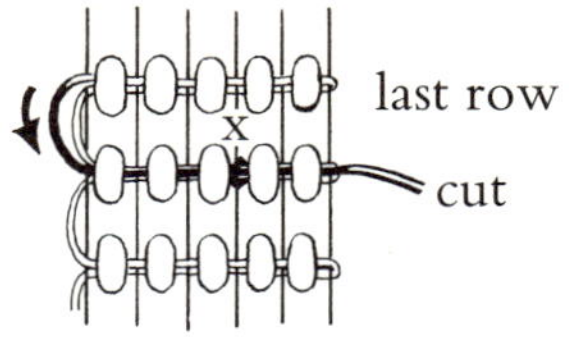

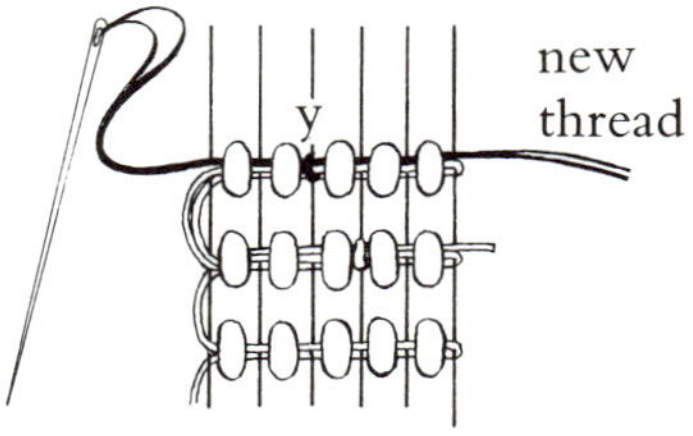

adding new thread

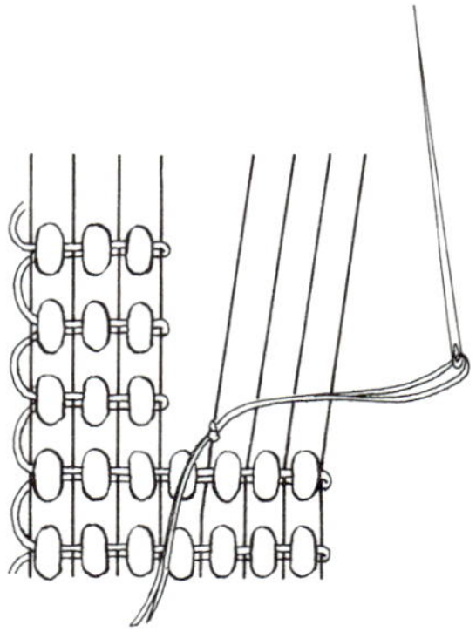

(*above left*): Concealing old thread
(*left*): Dividing beadwork

(*right*): The dividing point in a loom necklace

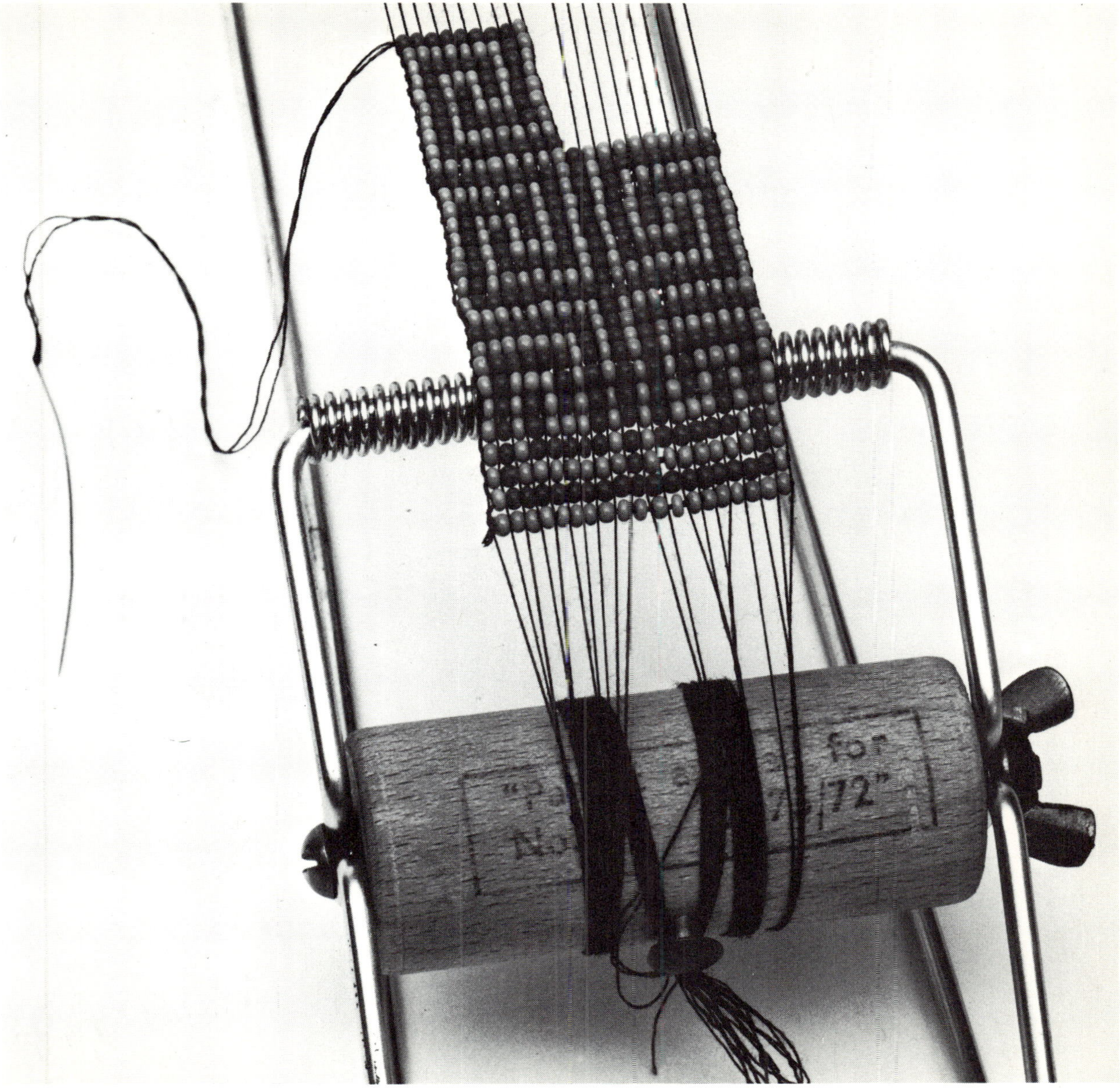

Finishing processes

Fringing

Two warp threads are used for each strand of fringe.
Thread needle on to end of outside warp thread (left of bead A).
Pass needle through bead B and down through all the other beads to bead C.
After picking up beads D come back up again through bead C and also through all the other beads and knot onto the next warp thread at E.
Weave ends of warp threads into work. All the other fringe strands are made in a similar manner.
For a close fringe, thread the beads onto each *warp* thread. Pass the needle back through all the beads except the last three threaded. Work each warp thread back into the necklace, securing with a slip knot (see Chapter 3). After making a slip knot, always pass the needle through a few beads before cutting the thread.

Concealing warp thread on finished work

This method is used when a neat edge is desired and the work is intended to be reversible.
Remove the work from the loom and lay it on a flat surface.

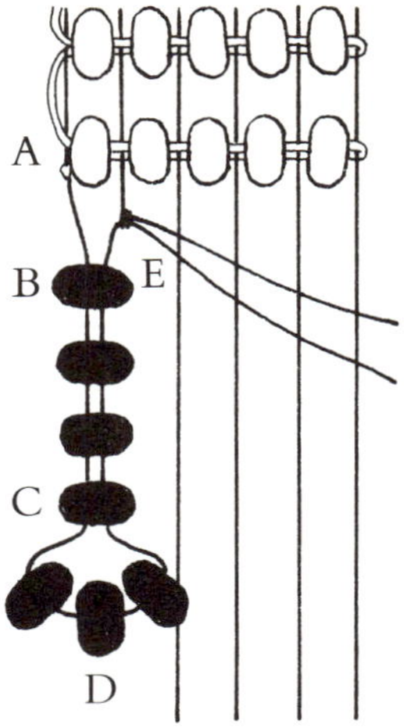

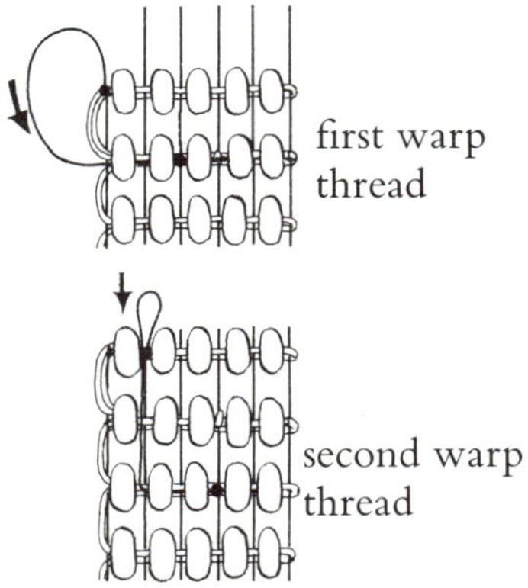

(*top*): Finishing: fringing

(*below*): Concealing warp threads

Thread the needle onto the first warp thread and knot this thread with the weaving thread to the left of bead A in the figure below. Pass the needle through several beads of the next row and make a knot at point B as illustrated.
Cut off the thread to the left of bead C in the figure.
All other warp threads are similarly woven back into the work.

Finishing a belt, choker, or bracelet

This method is used when the work is going to be mounted on materials such as felt, leather, ribbon, or when the edges are going to be attached to *Velcro*.
Finish off at both ends with selvedge, made by weaving a thread in and out of the warp threads, like darning.
The selvedge is pasted over with gum paper, or adhesive tape, and turned under the work when attaching to the belt or other piece of work.

To finish the back of the necklace

This is a two-man job! Remove the beadwork from the loom. One person holds the two right sides together, while the helper takes a pair of warp threads (one from each side) and ties them tightly together, twice. Cut 13 mm ($\frac{1}{2}$ in.) from the knot. Repeat this process with each successive pair of warp threads. Smooth a little glue over these knots and press a small strip of felt onto the beads to hide the joint.

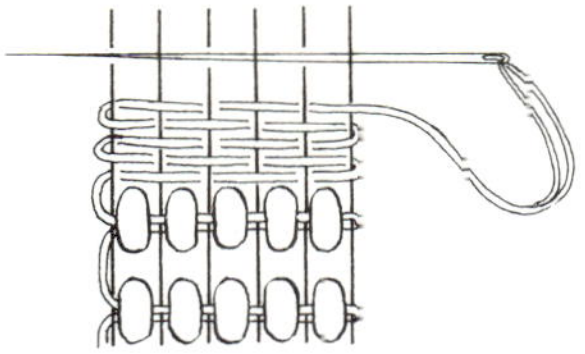

A more elaborate and neater method is to thread each warp thread in turn onto a needle and work it into the opposite end of the necklace. Secure each thread with a slip knot, as shown in Chapter 3.

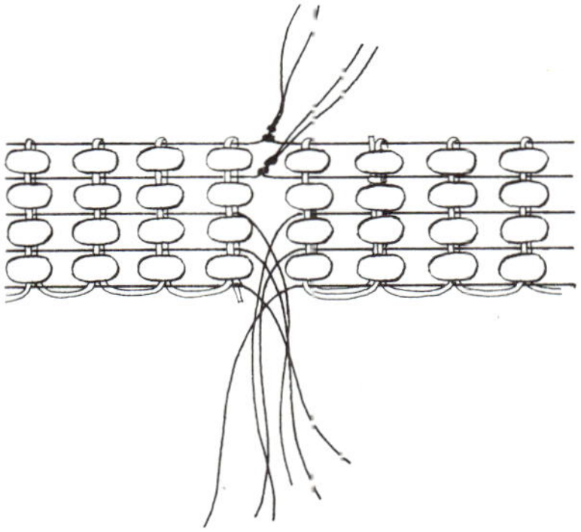

Fringing on the sides of beadwork
This finish is shown on Patterns 30 and 31.

To make a 6-bead side fringe, tie the weaving thread onto the first left-hand warp thread, and string a row of beads in the usual way, according to the pattern, but adding 6 extra beads to make the fringe. When turning at the end of the row, ignore the *sixth* bead, but thread the weaving thread back through the 5 fringe beads, *then* work through the pattern beads in the normal way.

Continue in this manner until the required number of fringes has been worked, and then continue the main strip of beadwork on the warp threads.

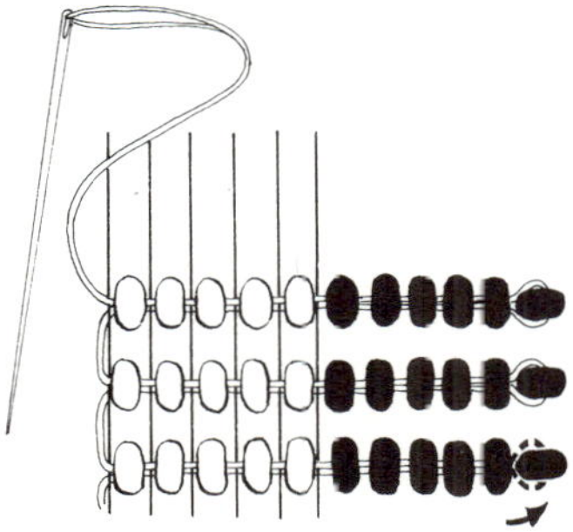

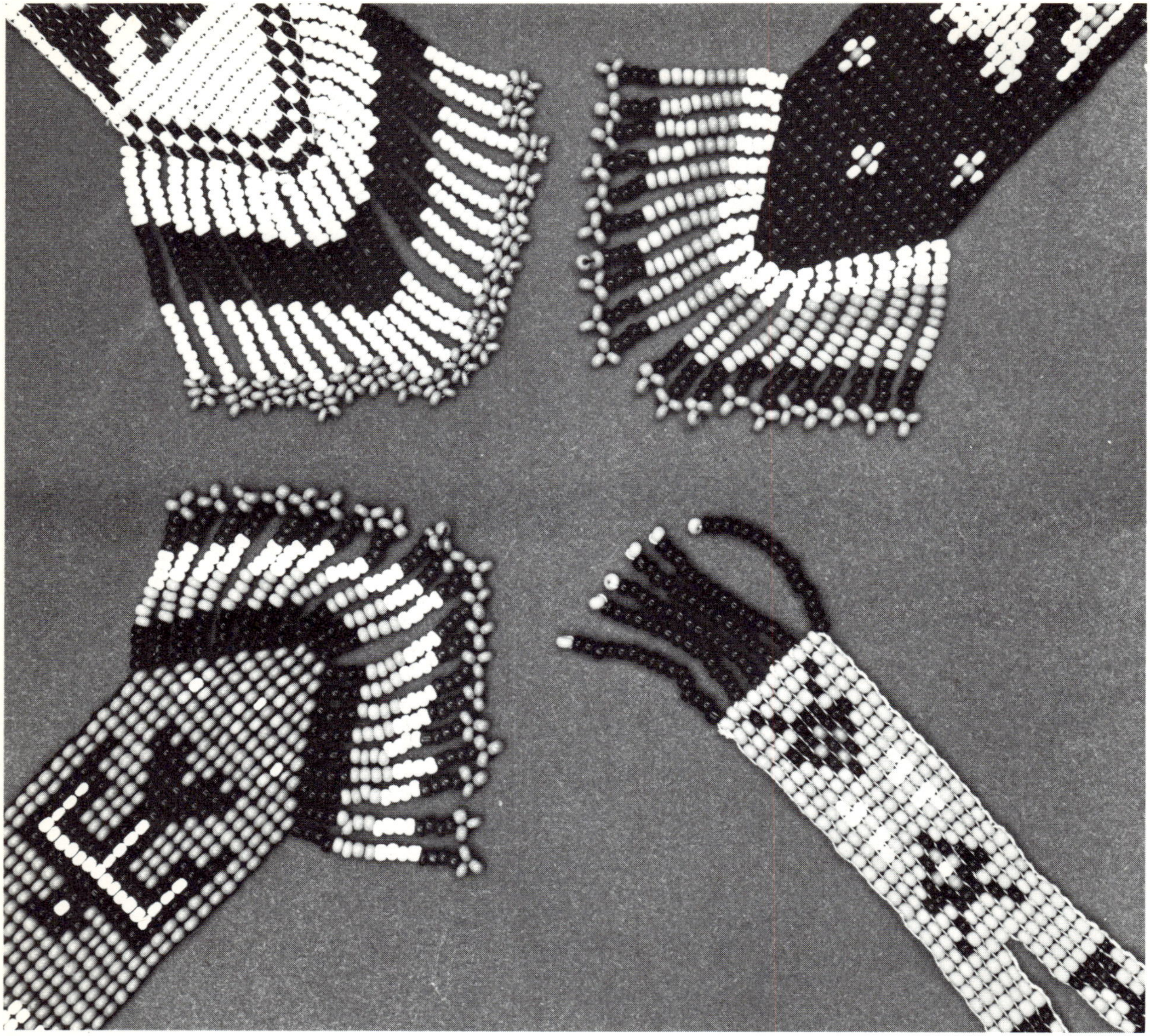

Endings for loom necklaces

7 Patterns for the loom

This chapter gives several patterns for making necklaces, headbands, belts, chokers, or bracelets. The various details for setting up the loom, finishing off work and so on, are not repeated with each pattern, but can be found in Chapters 5 and 6.

The materials required for the following patterns cannot be specifically given, as much depends on the length required by each individual maker. A reasonable starting point is that a 1 oz packet of size 2/0 beads is required for the main colour of an average length necklace. The best size of beading needle for these beads is number 10. *Drima* thread and treatment with beeswax are both recommended for the beadworking of all the following patterns.

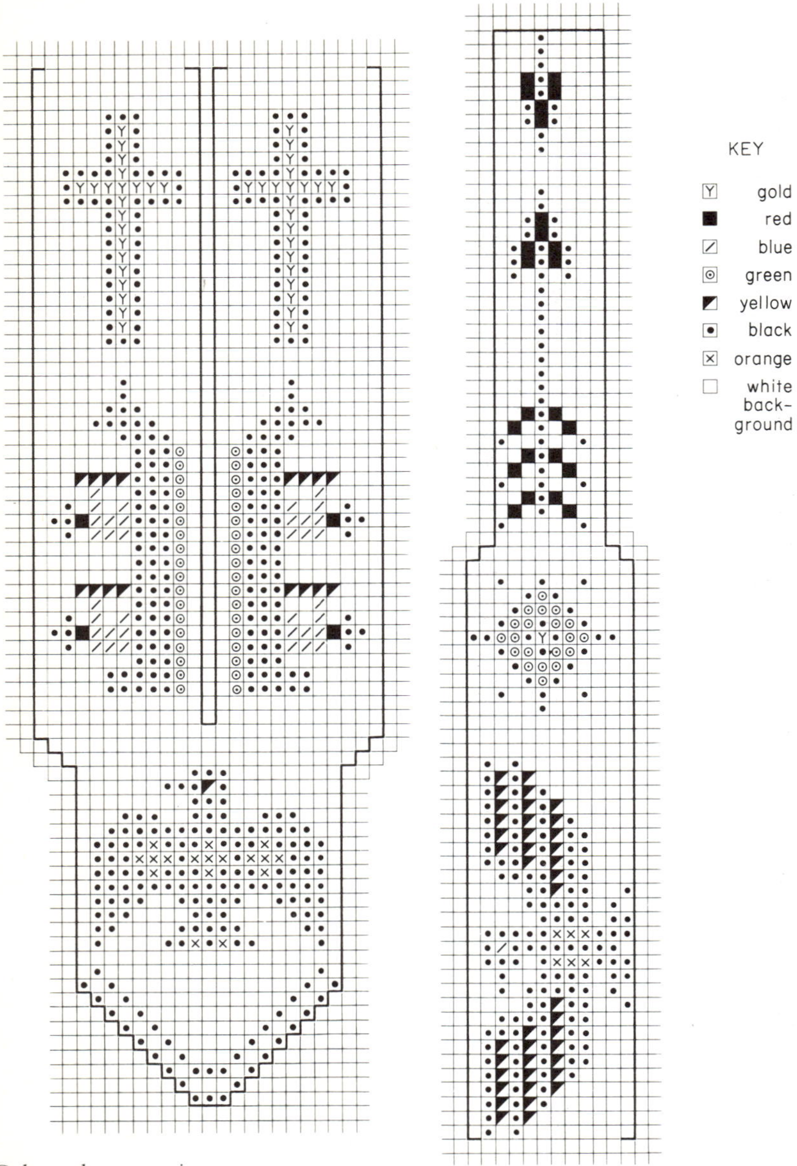

Colour plate opposite:
(*left*): Pattern 25 and (*right*): Pattern 23

PATTERN TWENTY-THREE

Necklace

Key
b = black w = white
y = yellow r = red
bl = blue g = green
go = gold o = orange

26 warp threads—start 12th space.

1 3b
2 1b 3w 1b
3 1b 1w 3b 1w 1b
4 1b 1w 1b 3w 1b 1w 1b
5 1b 1w 1b 5w 1b 1w 1b
6 1b 1w 1b 7w 1b 1w 1b
7 1b 1w 1b 9w 1b 1w 1b
8 1b 1w 1b 11w 1b 1w 1b
9 1b 1w 1b 13w 1b 1w 1b
10 1w 1b 15w 1b 1w
11 19w
12 1w 1b 4w 2b 1o 1b 1o 2b 4w 1b 1w
13 1w 2b 4w 5b 4w 2b 1w
14 1w 3b 4w 3b 4w 3b 1w
15 1w 4b 2w 5b 2w 4b 1w
16 1w 17b 1w
17 1w 4b 1o 3b 1o 3b 1o 4b 1w
18 1w 3b 3o 1b 3o 1b 3o 3b 1w
19 1w 4b 1o 3b 1o 3b 1o 4b 1w
20 2w 15b 2w
21 3w 3b 2w 3b 2w 3b 3w
22 8w 3b 8w
23 6w 3b 1y 1b 8w
24 8w 3b 8w

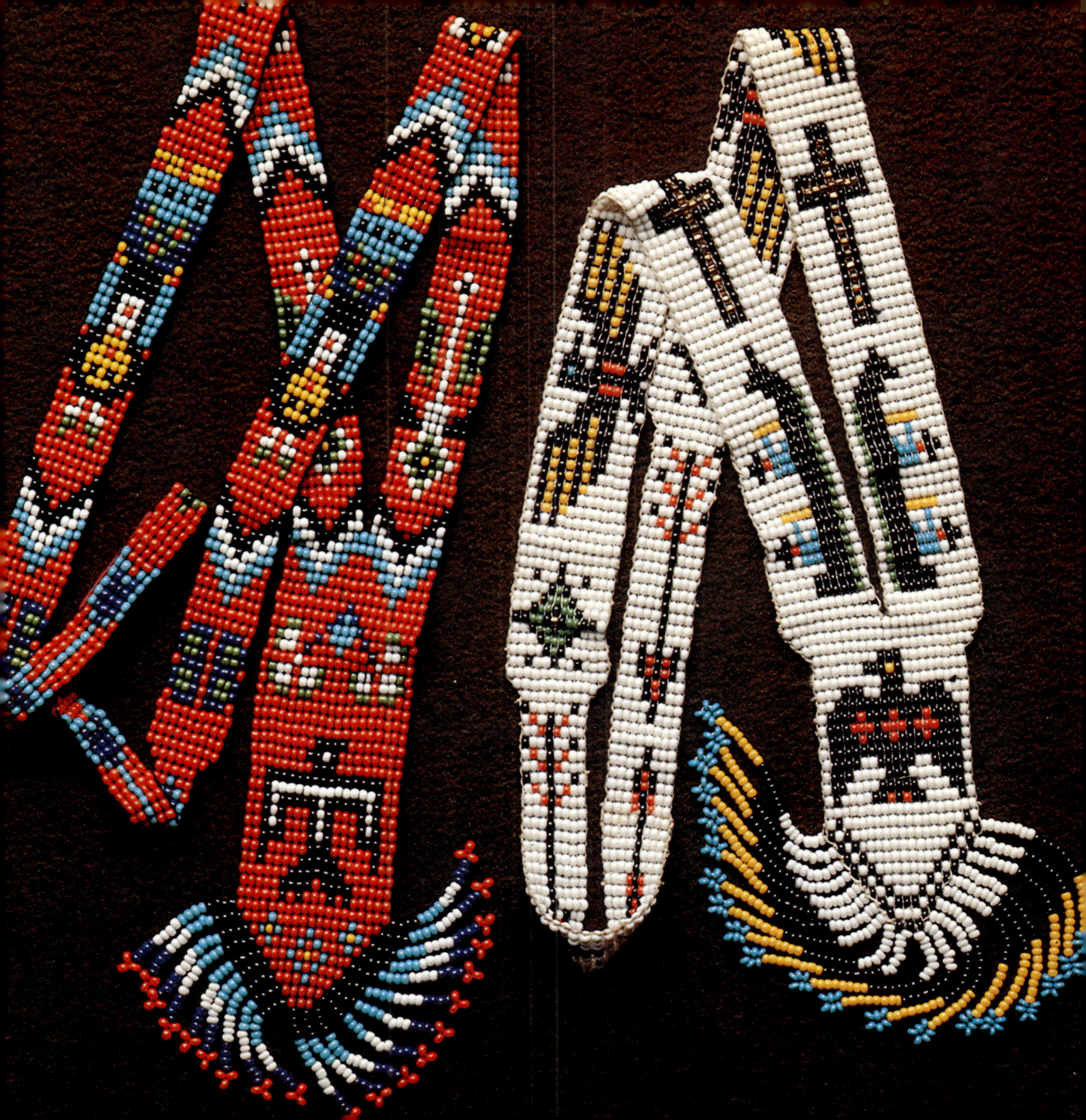

Widens

25 21w
26 23w
27 25w

Divide. Left side

28 12w
29 12w
30 5w 5b 1g 1w
31 5w 5b 1g 1w
32 7w 3b 1g 1w
33 2w 1b 1w 3bl 3b 1g 1w
34 1w 2b 1o 3bl 3b 1g 1w
35 2w 1b 1w 1bl 1w 1bl 3b 1g 1w
36 4w 1bl 2w 3b 1g 1w
37 3w 4y 3b 1g 1w
38 7w 3b 1g 1w
39 7w 3b 1g 1w
40 7w 3b 1g 1w
41 2w 1b 1w 3bl 3b 1g 1w
42 1w 2b 1o 3bl 3b 1g 1w
43 2w 1b 1w 1bl 1w 1bl 3b 1g 1w
44 4w 1bl 2w 3b 1g 1w
45 3w 4y 3b 1g 1w
46 7w 3b 1g 1w
47 7w 3b 1g 1w
48 6w 4b 2w
49 4w 5b 3w
50 5w 3b 4w
51 6w 1b 5w
52 6w 1b 5w
53 12w
54 12w
55 5w 3b 4w
56 5w 1b 1go 1b 4w
57 5w 1b 1go 1b 4w
58 5w 1b 1go 1b 4w (repeat 6 more times)
65 2w 4b 1go 4b 1w
66 2w 1b 7go 1b 1w
67 2w 4b 1go 4b 1w
68 5w 1b 1go 1b 4w
69 5w 1b 1go 1b 4w
70 5w 1b 1go 1b 4w
71 5w 3b 4w
72 12w
73 12w
74 12w
75 1w 1b 1w 1b 8w
76 1w 1b 1y 1b 1y 7w
77 1w 1b 1y 1b 1y 1b 6w
78 1w 1b 1y 1b 1y 1b 1y 5w
79 1w 1b 1y 1b 1y 1b 1y 1b 4w
80 1w 1b 1y 1b 1y 1b 1y 2b 3w
81 1w 1b 1y 1b 1y 1b 1y 2b 3w
82 1w 3b 1y 1b 1y 2b 3w
83 2w 4b 1y 2b 3w
84 4w 2b 1y 2b 2w 1b
85 2w 1b 1w 5b 1w 1b 1w
86 2w 1b 2w 4b 1w 2b
87 1w 3b 1w 1b 3o 3b
88 1w 1b 1bl 8b 1w
89 1w 5b 3o 3b
90 5w 4b 1w 2b
91 4w 5b 1w 1b 1w
92 4w 2b 1y 2b 2w 1b
93 2w 4b 1y 2b 3w
94 1w 3b 1y 1b 1y 2b 3w
95 1w 1b 1y 1b 1y 1b 1y 2b 3w
96 1w 1b 1y 1b 1y 1b 1y 2b 3w
97 1w 1b 1y 1b 1y 1b 1y 1b 4w
98 1w 1b 1y 1b 1y 1b 1y 5w
99 1w 1b 1y 1b 1y 1b 6w
100 1w 1b 1y 1b 1y 7w
101 1w 1b 1w 1b 8w
102 12w
103 5w 1b 6w
104 2w 1b 2w 1b 2w 1b 3w
105 4w 1b 1g 1b 5w
106 3w 1b 3g 1b 4w
107 2w 1b 2g 1b 2g 1b 3w
108 2b 2g 1b 1go 1b 2g 2b 1w
109 2w 1b 2g 1b 2g 1b 3w
110 3w 1b 3g 1b 4w
111 4w 1b 1g 1b 5w
112 2w 1b 2w 1b 2w 1b 3w
113 12w

Narrow

114 10w
115 8w
116 1b 5w 1b 1w
117 1w 1r 1w 1b 1w 1r 2w
118 2w 1r 1b 1r 3w
119 1b 2w 1b 2w 1b 1w
120 1w 1r 1w 1b 1w 1r 2w
121 2w 1r 1b 1r 3w
122 1b 2w 1b 2w 1b 1w
123 1w 1r 1w 1b 1w 1r 2w
124 2w 1r 1b 1r 3w
125 3w 1b 4w (do 9 times)
134 1w 1b 1w 1b 1w 1b 2w
135 1w 1b 1r 1b 1r 1b 2w

136 1w 1b 1r 1b 1r 1b 2w
137 2w 1b 1r 1b 3w
138 2w 1b 1r 1b 3w
139 3w 1b 4w
140 3w 1b 4w
141 8w (2 rows)
143 3w 1b 4w
144 3w 1b 4w
145 2w 1b 1r 1b 3w
146 2w 1b 1r 1b 3w
147 2w 1r 1b 1r 3w
148 2w 1r 1b 1r 3w
149 3w 1b 4w (do 3 times)

Reverse the pattern for the right side.
Fasten the thread off in the next to the last row using slip knots (see Chapter 3).

The fringe
Each strand has: 8w 8b 8y 6bl.

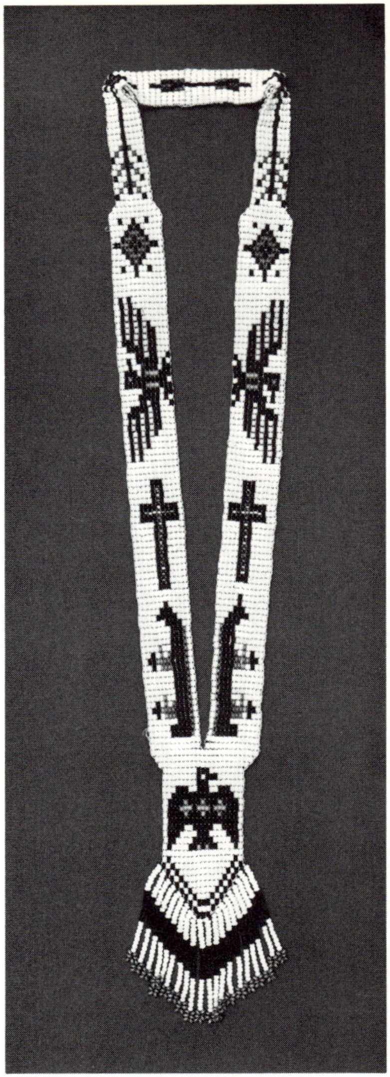

Pattern 23

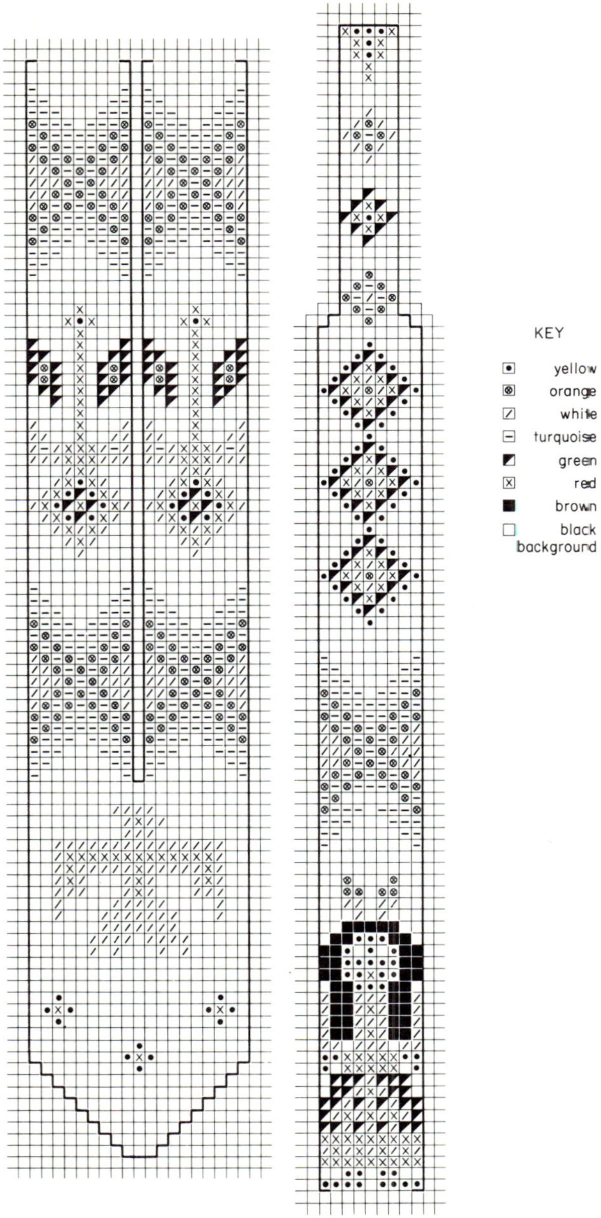

PATTERN TWENTY-FOUR

Necklace

Key
B = Black   Y = Yellow
R = Red   W = White
T = Turquoise   o = Orange
G = Light green
BRW = Brown

20 Warp threads
1 (9th space) 3B
2 5B
3 7B
4 9B
5 11B
6 13B
7 15B
8 8B 1Y 8B
9 8B 1Y 1R 1Y 8B
10 9B 1Y 9B
11 19B
12 2B 1Y 13B 1Y 2B
13 1B 1Y 1R 1Y 11B 1Y 1R 1Y 1B
14 2B 1Y 13B 1Y 2B
15 19B (3 rows)
18 5B 1W 1B 1W 3B 1W 1B 1W 5B
19 5B 4W 1B 4W 5B
20 6B 7W 6B
21 2B 1W 3B 7W 3B 1W 2B
22 2B 1W 4B 5W 4B 1W 2B
23 2B 3W 3B 1W 1R 1W 3B 3W 2B

24 2B 1W 1R 1W 3B 1W 1R 1W 3B 1W 1R 1W 2B
25 2B 1W 1R 5W 1R 5W 1R 1W 2B
26 2B 1W 13R 1W 2B
27 2B 15W 2B
28 8B 3W 8B
29 7B 2W 1R 1W 8B
30 8B 4W 7B
31 19B (2 rows)

Divide. One side
33 1T 7B 1T
34 2T 5B 2T
35 3T 3B 3T
36 1O 3T 1B 3T 1O
37 1T 1O 5T 1O 1T
38 1O 1T 1O 3T 1O 1T 1O
39 1W 1O 1T 1O 1T 1O 1T 1O 1W
40 2W 1O 1T 1O 1T 1O 2W
41 3W 1O 1T 1O 3W
42 2W 1O 1T 1O 1T 1O 2W
43 1W 1O 1T 1O 1T 1O 1T 1O 1W
44 1O 1T 1O 3T 1O 1T 1O
45 1T 1O 5T 1O 1T
46 1O 3T 1B 3T 1O
47 3T 3B 3T
48 2T 5B 2T
49 1T 7B 1T
50 9B (2 rows)
52 4B 1W 4B
53 3B 1W 1R 1W 3B
54 2B 1W 1R 1W 1R 1W 2B
55 1B 1W 1R 1Y 1G 1Y 1R 1W 1B
56 1W 1R 1Y 1G 1R 1G 1Y 1R 1W
57 1B 1W 1R 1Y 1G 1Y 1R 1W 1B
58 2B 1W 1R 1Y 1R 1W 2B
59 3B 1W 1R 1W 3B
60 3W 3R 3W
61 1W 1T 1W 3R 1W 1T 1W
62 2W 2B 1R 2B 2W
63 1W 3B 1R 3B 1W
64 4B 1R 4B
65 2B 1G 1B 1R 1B 1G 2B
66 1B 2G 1B 1R 1B 2G 1B
67 1G 1O 1G 1B 1R 1B 1G 1O 1G
68 1G 1O 1G 1B 1R 1B 1G 1O 1G
69 2G 2B 1R 2B 2G
70 1G 3B 1R 3B 1G
71 4B 1R 4B
72 3B 1R 1Y 1R 3B
73 4B 1R 4B
74 9B (2 rows)
76 1T 7B 1T
77 2T 5B 2T
78 3T 3B 3T
79 1O 3T 1B 3T 1O
80 1T 1O 5T 1O 1T
81 1O 1T 1O 3T 1O 1T 1O
82 1W 1O 1T 1O 1T 1O 1T 1O 1W
83 2W 1O 1T 1O 1T 1O 2W
84 3W 1O 1T 1O 3W
85 2W 1O 1T 1O 1T 1O 2W
86 1W 1O 1T 1O 1T 1O 1T 1O 1W
87 1O 1T 1O 3T 1O 1T 1O
88 1T 1O 5T 1O 1T
89 1O 3T 1B 3T 1O
90 3T 3B 3T
91 2T 5B 2T
92 1T 7B 1T
93 9B (2 rows)
95 4Y 1B 4Y
96 2B 2Y 1B 2Y 2B
97 9R
98 1W 1R 1W 1R 1W 1R 1W 1R 1W
99 9R
100 2G 1W 1G 1W 1G 1W 2G
101 1G 1W 1R 1W 1R 1W 1R 1W 1G
102 2G 1W 1G 1W 1G 1W 2G
103 1B 2G 1W 1R 1W 2G 1B
104 1B 3G 1W 3G 1B
105 1Y 1B 5R 1B 1Y
106 2Y 5R 2Y
107 2W 1B 3W 1B 2W
108 1W 2BRW 1W 1R 1W 2BRW 1W
109 1W 2BRW 3W 2BRW 1W
110 1W 2BRW 1W 1R 1W 2BRW 1W
111 1W 2BRW 3W 2BRW 1W
112 1B 2BRW 3Y 2BRW 1B
113 2BRW 2Y 1R 2Y 2BRW
114 2BRW 5Y 2BRW

115 2BRW 1Y 1B 1Y 1B 1Y
2BRW
116 1B 2BRW 3Y 2BRW 1B
117 2B 5BRW 2B
118 3B 1W 1B 1W 3B
119 2B 2W 1B 2W 2B
120 2B 2O 1B 2O 2B
121 2B 1O 3B 1O 2B
122 9B (2 rows)
124 1T 7B 1T
125 2T 5B 2T
126 3T 3B 3T
127 1O 3T 1B 3T 1O
128 1T 1O 5T 1O 1T
129 1O 1T 1O 3T 1O 1T 1O
130 1W 1O 1T 1O 1T 1O 1T
1O 1W
131 2W 1O 1T 1O 1T 1O 2W
132 3W 1O 1T 1O 3W
133 2W 1O 1T 1O 1T 1O 2W
134 1W 1O 1T 1O 1T 1O 1T
1O 1W
135 1O 1T 1O 3T 1O 1T 1O
136 1T 1O 5T 1O 1T
137 1O 3T 1B 3T 1O
138 3T 3B 3T
139 2T 5B 2T
140 1T 7B 1T
141 9B (2 rows)
143 4B 1Y 4B
144 3B 1Y 1G 1Y 3B
145 2B 1Y 1G 1R 1G 1Y 2B
146 1B 1Y 1G 1R 1W 1R
1G 1Y 1B
147 1Y 1G 1R 1W 1O 1W
1R 1G 1Y
148 1B 1Y 1G 1R 1W 1R
1G 1Y 1B

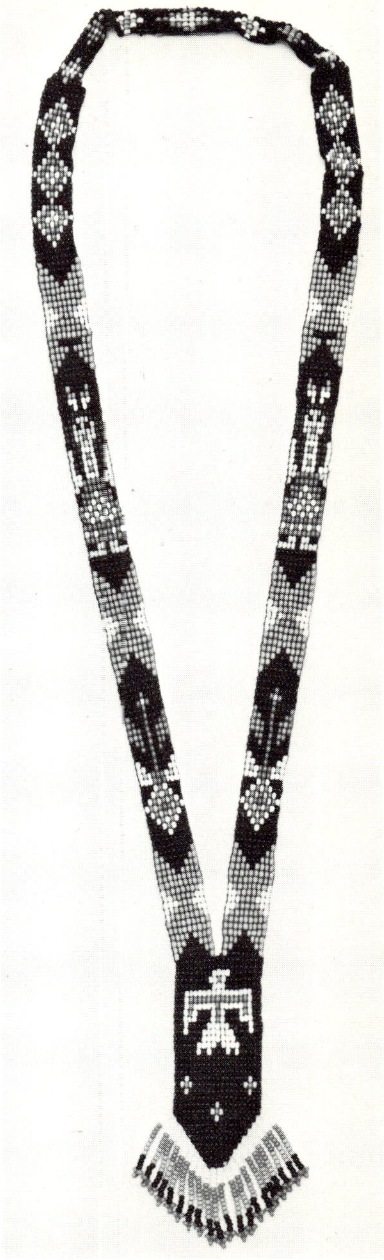

Pattern 24

149 2B 1Y 1G 1R 1G 1Y 2B
150 3B 1Y 1G 1Y 3B
151 4B 1Y 4B
152 3B 1Y 1G 1Y 3B
153 2B 1Y 1G 1R 1G 1Y 2B
154 1B 1Y 1G 1R 1W 1R
1G 1Y 1B
155 1Y 1G 1R 1W 10 1W
1R 1G 1Y
156 1B 1Y 1G 1R 1W 1R
1G 1Y 1B
157 2B 1Y 1G 1R 1G 1Y 2B
158 3B 1Y 1G 1Y 3B
159 4B 1Y 4B
160 3B 1Y 1G 1Y 3B
161 2B 1Y 1G 1R 1G 1Y 2B
162 1B 1Y 1G 1R 1W 1R
1G 1Y 1B
163 1Y 1G 1R 1W 10 1W
1R 1G 1Y
164 1B 1Y 1G 1R 1W 1R
1G 1Y 1B
165 2B 1Y 1G 1R 1G 1Y 2B
166 3B 1Y 1G 1Y 3B
167 4B 1Y 4B
168 9B (2 rows)

Narrow
170 3B 10 3B
171 1B 10 1T 10 1B
172 10 1T 1W 1T 10
173 1B 10 1T 10 1B
174 2B 10 2B
175 5B (2 rows)
177 2B 1G 2B
178 1B 1G 1R 1G 1B
179 1G 1R 1Y 1R 1G
180 1B 1G 1R 1G 1B
181 2B 1G 2B
182 5B (2 rows)
184 2B 1W 2B
185 1B 1W 10 1W 1B
186 1W 10 1T 10 1W
187 1B 1W 10 1W 1B
188 2B 1W 2B
189 5B (2 rows)
191 2B 1R 2B (2 rows)
193 1B 1R 1Y 1R 1B
(2 rows)
195 1R 3Y 1R

Fasten the thread into the next to the last row using slip knots (see chapter 3).
Repeat Rows 33–195 for right-hand side.

Fringe
Thread 4W 4R 4T 4B 3R.

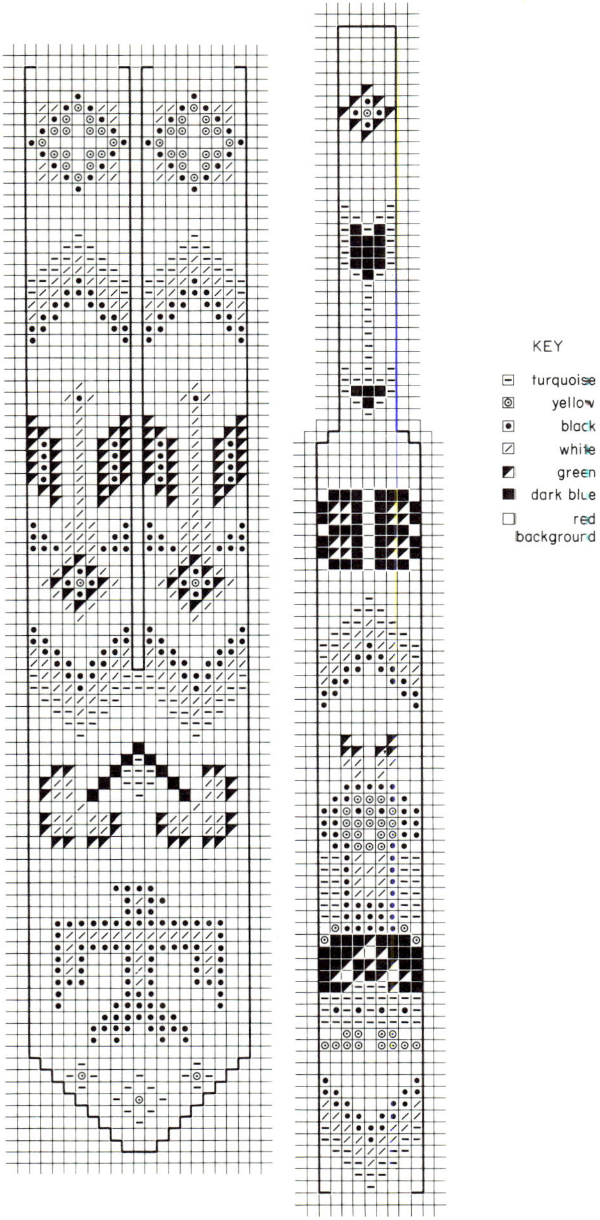

PATTERN TWENTY-FIVE

Necklace

Key

r = red t = turquoise
y = yellow b = black
w = white g = green
dk.bl = dark blue

20 Warp Threads 19 beads
Starting 9th Space

1 3r
2 5r
3 3r 1t 3r
4 3r 1t 1r 1t 3r
5 3r 1t 1r 1y 1r 1t 3r
6 1r 1t 3r 1t 1r 1t 3r 1t 1r
7 1r 1t 1y 1t 3r 1t 3r 1t 1y 1t 1r
8 3r 1t 9r 1t 3r
9 19r
10 5r 1b 1r 1b 3r 1b 1r 1b 5r
11 5r 4b 1r 4b 5r
12 6r 7b 6r
13 2r 1b 4r 5b 4r 1b 2r
14 2r 1b 5r 3b 5r 1b 2r
15 2r 3b 3r 1b 1w 1b 3r 3b 2r
16 2r 1b 1w 1b 3r 1b 1w 1b 3r 1b 1w 1b 2r
17 2r 1b 1w 1b 3r 1b 1w 1b 3r 1b 1w 1b 2r
18 2r 1b 1w 5b 1w 5b 1w 1b 2r
19 2r 1b 13w 1b 2r
20 2r 15b 2r
21 8r 3b 8r

22 8r 1b 1w 2b 7r
23 7r 4b 8r
24 19r (three times)
27 2r 2g 1r 2g 5r 2g 1r 2g 2r
28 1r 1g 2w 1r 2w 1g 3r 1g 2w 1r 2w 1g 1r
29 1r 1g 2w 1r 2w 1g 3r 1g 2w 1r 2w 1g 1r
30 4r 1w 9r 1w 4r
31 1r 1g 2w 1r 1dk.bl 3r 1t 3r 1dk.bl 1r 2w 1g 1r
32 1r 1g 2w 2r 1dk.bl 1r 3t 1r 1dk.bl 2r 2w 1g 1r
33 2r 2g 3r 1dk.bl 3t 1dk.bl 3r 2g 2r
34 8r 1dk.bl 1t 1dk.bl 8r
35 9r 1dk.bl 9r
36 4r 1t 9r 1t 4r
37 3r 3t 7r 3t 3r
38 2r 2t 1w 2t 5r 2t 1w 2t 2r
39 1r 2t 3w 2t 3r 2t 3w 2t 1r
40 2t 2w 1b 2w 5t 2w 1b 2w 2t
41 1t 2w 3b 2w 3t 2w 3b 2w 1t

Divide. One side
42 2w 2b 1r 2b 2w
43 1w 2b 3r 2b 1w
44 2b 5r 2b
45 1b 7r 1b
46 4r 1w 4r
47 3r 1w 1g 1w 3r
48 2r 1w 1g 1b 1g 1w 2r
49 1r 1w 1g 1b 1y 1b 1g 1w 1r
50 2r 1w 1g 1b 1g 1w 2r
51 3r 1w 1g 1w 3r
52 3b 3w 3b
53 2b 1r 3w 1r 2b
54 1b 2r 3w 2r 1b
55 4r 1w 4r
56 2r 1g 1r 1w 1r 1g 2r
57 1r 2g 1r 1w 1r 2g 1r
58 1g 1b 1g 1r 1w 1r 1g 1b 1g (4 rows)
62 2g 2r 1w 2r 2g
63 1g 3r 1w 3r 1g
64 4r 1w 4r
65 3r 1w 1b 1w 3r
66 4r 1w 4r
67 9r (3 rows)
70 1b 7r 1b
71 2b 5r 2b
72 1w 2b 3r 2b 1w
73 2w 2b 1r 2b 2w
74 1t 2w 3b 2w 1t
75 2t 2w 1b 2w 2t
76 1r 2t 3w 2t 1r
77 2r 2t 1w 2t 2r
78 3r 3t 3r
79 4r 1t 4r
80 9r (3 rows)
83 4r 1b 4r
84 1r 2w 1b 1y 1b 2w 1r
85 1r 1w 1b 1y 1r 1y 1b 1w 1r
86 1r 1b 2y 1r 2y 1b 1r
87 1b 1y 5r 1y 1b
88 1r 1b 2y 1r 2y 1b 1r
89 1r 1w 1b 1y 1r 1y 1b 1w 1r
90 1r 2w 1b 1y 1b 2w 1r
91 4r 1b 4r
92 9r (2 rows)
94 4r 1t 4r
95 3r 3t 3r
96 2r 2t 1w 2t 2r
97 1r 2t 3w 2t 1r
98 2t 2w 1b 2w 2t
99 1t 2w 3b 2w 1t
100 2w 2b 1r 2b 2w
101 1w 2b 3r 2b 1w
102 2b 5r 2b
103 1b 7r 1b
104 9r (2 rows)
106 4y 1r 4y
107 2r 2y 1r 2y 2r
108 9t
109 1t 1b 1t 1b 1t 1b 1t 1b 1t
110 9t
111 2dk.bl 1g 3t 1g 2dk.bl
112 1dk.bl 1g 1r 1g 1dk.bl 1g 1r 1g 1dk.bl
113 2dk.bl 1g 1dk.bl 1g 1dk.bl 1g 2dk.bl
114 3dk.bl 1g 1r 1g 3dk.bl
115 1y 3dk.bl 1g 3dk.bl 1y
116 1r 1y 5b 1y 1r
117 2t 5b 2t (2 rows)
119 2t 1b 3w 1b 2t
120 2t 1b 1w 1r 1w 1b 2t
121 2t 1b 3w 1b 2t
122 2t 1b 1w 1r 1w 1b 2t
123 1r 2b 3y 2b 1r
124 2b 2y 1r 2y 2b
125 2b 5y 2b
126 2b 1y 1b 1y 1b 1y 2b
127 1r 2b 3y 2b 1r
128 2r 5b 2r
129 3r 1w 1r 1w 3r
130 2r 2w 1r 2w 2r

131 2r 2g 1r 2g 2r
132 2r 1g 3r 1g 2r
133 9r (2 rows)
135 1b 7r 1b
136 2b 5r 2b
137 1w 2b 3r 2b 1w
138 2w 2b 1r 2b 2w
139 1t 2w 3b 2w 1t
140 2t 2w 1b 2w 2t
141 1r 2t 3w 2t 1r
142 2r 2t 1w 2t 2r
143 3r 3t 3r
144 4r 1t 4r
145 9r (2 rows)
147 1r 3dk.bl 1r 3dk.bl 1r
148 1dk.bl 2g 1dk.bl 1r
1dk.bl 2g 1dk.bl
(2 rows)
150 1r 3dk.bl 1r 3dk.bl 1r
151 1dk.bl 2g 1dk.bl 1r
1dk.bl 2g 1dk.bl
(2 rows)
153 1r 3dk.bl 1r 3dk.bl 1r
154 9r (4 rows)

Narrow
158 7r
159 5r
160 2r 1t 2r
161 1r 1t 1dk.bl 1t 1r
162 1t 3dk.bl 1t
163 5t
164 1t 1r 1t 1r 1t
165 2r 1t 2r (7 rows)
172 1r 1t 1dk.bl 1t 1r
173 1t 3dkbl 1t (3 times)
176 1t 1dk.bl 1t 1dk.bl 1t
177 2t 1r 2t
178 1t 3r 1t
179 5r (5 rows)
184 2r 1g 2r
185 1r 1g 1b 1g 1r
186 1g 1b 1y 1b 1g
187 1r 1g 1b 1g 1r
188 2r 1g 2r
189 5r (5 rows)

Fasten the thread into the next but last row using slip knots (see Chapter 3).
Repeat Rows 42–194 for the right side.

Fringe
Thread 4b
4t
4w
4dk.bl
3r

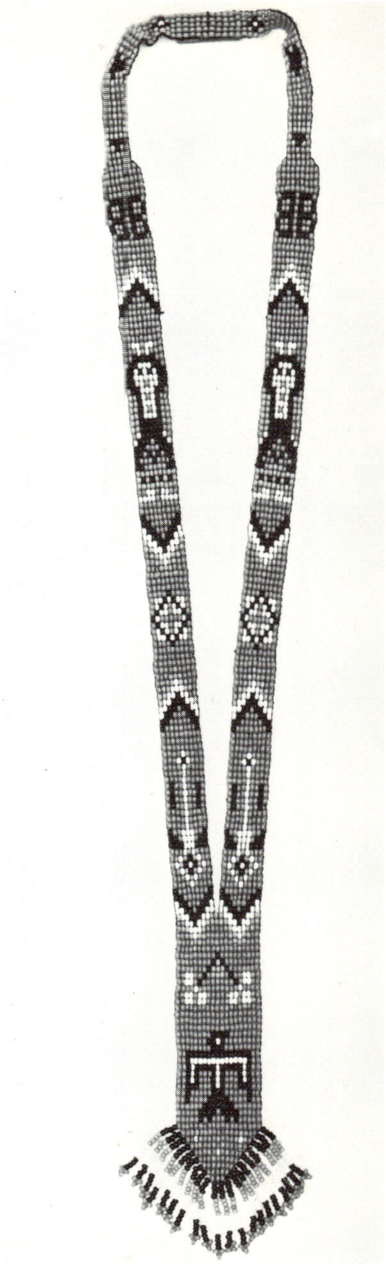

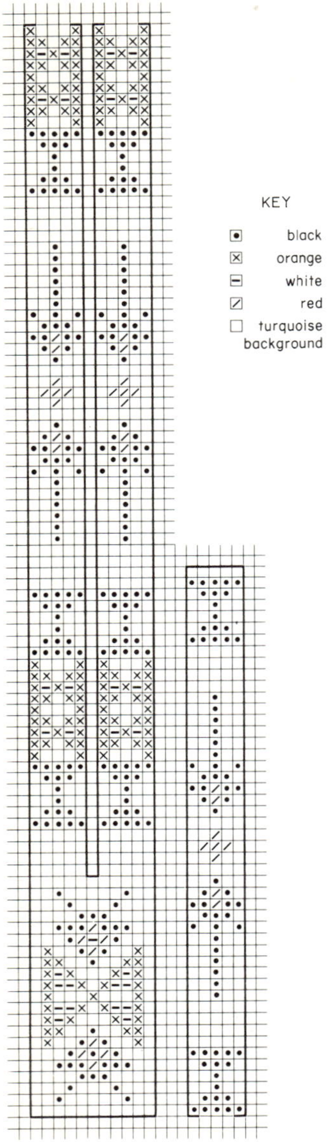

PATTERN TWENTY-SIX Child's necklace.

Key
t = turquoise b = black
o = orange w = white
r = red

12 Warp threads 11 beads
1 11t
2 2t 1b 5t 1b 2t
3 3t 1b 3t 1b 3t
4 4t 3b 4t
5 2t 3b 1r 3b 2t
6 3t 1b 1r 1b 1r 1b 3t
7 1t 1o 2t 1b 1r 1b 2t 1o 1t
8 1t 2o 2t 1b 2t 2o 1t
9 1t 1o 1w 1o 3t 1o 1w 1o 1t
10 1t 1o 2w 1o 1t 1o 2w 1o 1t
11 1t 1o 3t 1o 3t 1o 1t
12 1t 1o 2w 1o 1t 1o 2w 1o 1t
13 1t 1o 1w 1o 3t 1o 1w 1o 1t
14 1t 2o 2t 1b 2t 2o 1t
15 1t 1o 2t 1b 1r 1b 2t 1o 1t
16 3t 1b 1r 1w 1r 1b 3t
17 2t 3b 1r 3b 2t
18 4t 3b 4t
19 3t 1b 3t 1b 3t
20 2t 1b 5t 1b 2t
21 11t

Divide: work one side
22 5t (4 rows)
26 5b
27 1t 3b 1t
28 2t 1b 2t (2 rows)
30 1t 3b 1t
31 5b
32 1o 3t 1o
33 2o 1t 2o
34 1o 1w 1o 1w 1o
35 2o 1t 2o
36 1o 3t 1o
37 2o 1t 2o
38 1o 1w 1o 1w 1o
39 2o 1t 2o
40 1o 3t 1o
41 5b
42 1t 3b 1t
43 2t 1b 2t (2 rows)
45 1t 3b 1t
46 5b
47 5t (4 rows)
51 2t 1b 2t (6 rows)
57 1b 1t 1b 1t 1b
58 1t 3b 1t
59 2b 1r 2b
60 1t 1b 1r 1b 1t
61 2t 1b 2t
62 5t
63 2t 1r 2t
64 1t 3r 1t
65 2t 1r 2t
66 5t
67 2t 1b 2t
68 1t 1b 1r 1b 1t
69 2b 1r 2b
70 1t 3b 1t
71 1b 1t 1b 1t 1b
72 2t 1b 2t (6 rows)

Repeat from Row 22 until desired length is achieved.
Work the right-hand side to match.
Fasten the thread into the next to the last row using slip knots (see Chapter 3).

Fringe
Thread 16b 1t

PATTERN TWENTY-SEVEN
Corinthian Column Necklace.

Key
M = main colour
C = contrast colour

23 beads 24 threads

1 23M
2 1M 2C 1M 2C 1M 8C 1M 3C 1M 2C 1M
3 1M 2C 1M 2C 1M 8C 1M 3C 1M 2C 1M
4 3M 1C 3M 2C 4M 2C 4M 1C 3M
5 1M 2C 1M 2C 1M 2C 1M 2C 1M 2C 1M 3C 1M 2C 1M
6 1M 2C 1M 2C 1M 2C 1M 2C 1M 2C 1M 3C 1M 2C 1M
7 13M 2C 8M
8 1M 11C 1M 2C 1M 6C 1M
9 1M 11C 1M 2C 1M 6C 1M
10 1M 2C 10M 2C 5M 2C 1M
11 1M 2C 1M 2C 1M 2C 1M 2C 1M 2C 1M 3C 1M 2C 1M
12 1M 2C 1M 2C 1M 2C 1M 2C 1M 2C 1M 3C 1M 2C 1M
13 1M 2C 4M 2C 11M 2C 1M
14 1M 5C 1M 2C 1M 12C 1M
15 1M 5C 1M 2C 1M 12C 1M
16 7M 2C 14M
17 1M 2C 1M 2C 1M 2C 1M 3C 1M 2C 1M 2C 1M 2C 1M
18 1M 2C 1M 2C 1M 2C 1M 3C 1M 2C 1M 2C 1M 2C 1M
19 3M 1C 3M 2C 5M 2C 3M 1C 3M
20 1M 2C 1M 2C 1M 9C 1M 2C 1M 2C 1M

Divide. One side
21 7M 1C 1M 1C 1M
22 1M 7C 1M 1C 1M
23 1M 1C 7M 1C 1M
24 1M 1C 1M 1C 2M 1C 2M 1C 1M
25 1M 1C 1M 2C 1M 2C 1M 1C 1M
26 1M 1C 1M 7C 1M
27 1M 1C 1M 2C 1M 2C 1M 1C 1M
28 1M 1C 1M 1C 2M 1C 2M 1C 1M
29 1M 1C 7M 1C 1M
30 1M 1C 1M 7C 1M
31 1M 1C 1M 1C 7M
32 1M 1C 1M 1C 1M 5C 1M
33 1M 1C 1M 1C 1M 1C 3M 1C 1M
34 1M 1C 1M 5C 1M 1C 1M

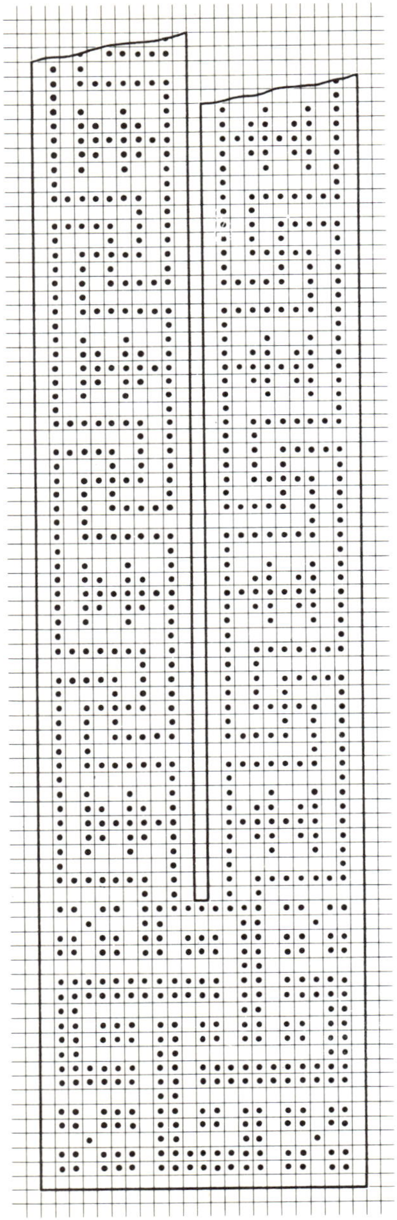

KEY

35 1M 1C 3M 1C 1M 1C
1M 1C 1M
36 1M 5C 1M 1C 1M 1C
1M

Repeat pattern from Row 21 until desired length is achieved. Work other side of necklace to match, but reverse the pattern. E.g.: 21 1M 1C 1M 1C 7M

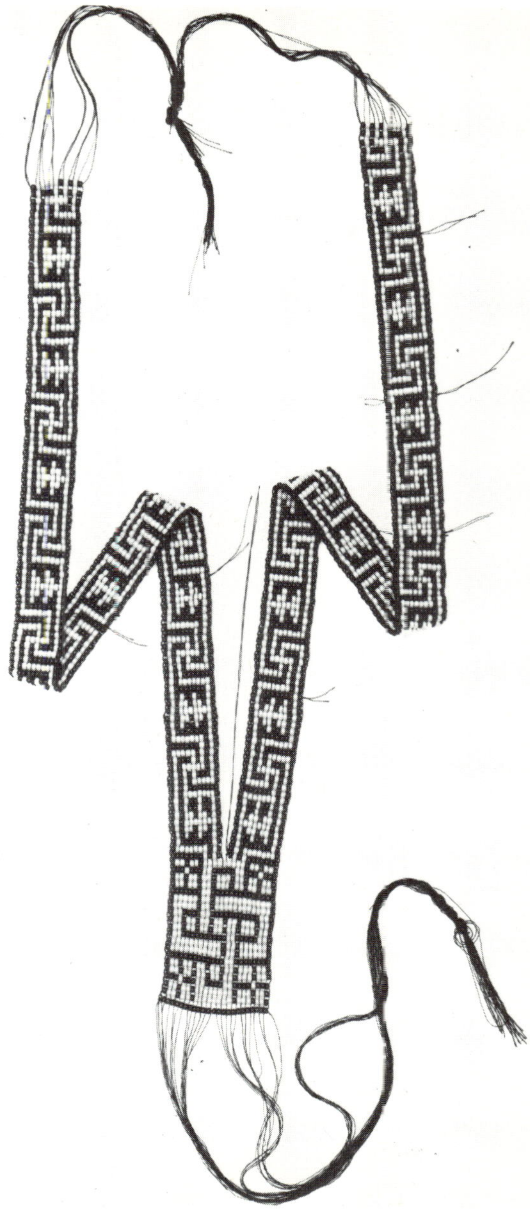

(*left*): Graph for Pattern 27
(*right*): Pattern 27: a necklace just removed from the loom

PATTERN TWENTY-EIGHT

Strip of beadwork.

Key

b = blue o = orange

w = white g = green

y = yellow bl = black

18 warp threads 17 beads

1 8b 1o 8b

2 7b 3o 7b

3 6b 2o 1w 2o 6b

4 5b 2o 1w 1g 1w 2o 5b

5 6o 1w 1g 1y 1g 1w 6o

6 1b 2o 3w 1g 1y 1bl 1y 1g 3w 2o 1b

7 2b 2o 1w 1g 1y 3bl 1y 1g 1w 2o 2b

8 3b 2o 1w 1g 1y 1bl 1y 1g 1w 2o 3b

9 4b 2o 1w 1g 1y 1g 1w 2o 4b

10 5b 2o 1w 1g 1w 2o 5b

11 6b 2o 1w 2o 6b

12 7b 3o 7b

13 1b 4y 3b 1o 3b 4y 1b

14 7b 3o 7b

15 6b 2o 1w 2o 6b

16 5b 2o 1w 1g 1w 2o 5b

17 4b 2o 1w 1g 1y 1g 1w 2o 4b

18 3b 2o 1w 1g 1y 1bl 1y 1g 1w 2o 3b

19 2b 2o 1w 1g 1y 3bl 1y 1g 1w 2o 2b

20 1b 2o 3w 1g 1y 1bl 1y 1g 3w 2o 1b

21 6o 1w 1g 1y 1g 1w 6o

22 5b 2o 1w 1g 1w 2o 5b

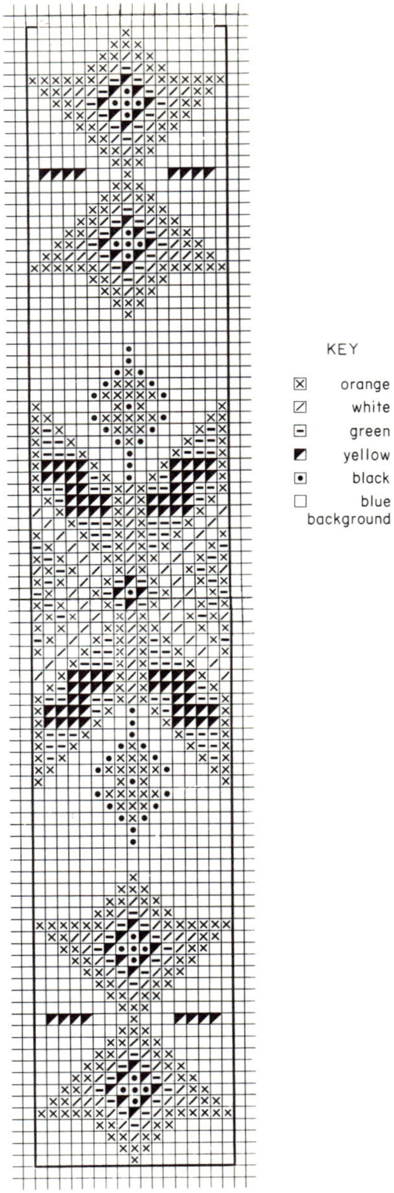

23 6b 2o 1w 2o 6b
24 7b 3o 7b
25 8b 1o 8b
26 17b (2 rows)
28 8b 1bl 8b (2 rows)
30 7b 1bl 1o 1bl 7b
31 6b 1bl 3o 1bl 6b
32 5b 1bl 5o 1bl 5b
33 1o 6b 1o 1bl 1o 6b 1o
34 2o 3b 1bl 5o 1bl 3b 2o
35 1o 1g 1o 3b 1bl 3o 1bl 3b 1o 1g 1o
36 1o 2g 1o 3b 1bl 1o 1bl 3b 1o 2g 1o
37 1o 3g 1o 3b 1bl 3b 1o 3g 1o
38 1o 4y 1o 2b 1bl 2b 1o 4y 1o
39 1o 4y 1g 1o 1b 1bl 1b 1o 1g 4y 1o
40 1o 2g 2y 2g 1o 1w 1o 2g 2y 2g 1o
41 1b 1o 1g 4y 1o 1w 1o 4y 1g 1o 1b
42 1w 1b 1o 4y 1o 1w 1o 4y 1o 1b 1w
43 1b 1w 1b 1o 3g 1o 1w 1o 3g 1o 1b 1w 1b
44 1o 1b 1w 1b 1o 2g 1o 1w 1o 2g 1o 1b 1w 1b 1o
45 1g 1o 1b 1w 1b 1o 1g 1o 1w 1o 1g 1o 1b 1w 1b 1o 1g
46 1o 1b 1o 1b 1w 1b 2o 1w 2o 1b 1w 1b 1o 1b 1o
47 1w 1o 1g 1o 1b 1w 1b 1o 1w 1o 1b 1w 1b 1o 1g 1o 1w
48 1o 1g 1o 1b 1w 1b 1o 1g 1y 1g 1o 1b 1w 1b 1o 1g 1o
49 1g 1o 1b 1w 1b 1o 1g 1y 1bl 1y 1g 1o 1b 1w 1b 1o 1g
50 1o 1g 1o 1b 1w 1b 1o 1g 1y 1g 1o 1b 1w 1b 1o 1g 1o
51 1w 1o 1g 1o 1b 1w 1b 1o 1w 1o 1b 1w 1b 1o 1g 1o 1w
52 1o 1g 1o 1b 1w 1b 2o 1w 2o 1b 1w 1b 1o 1g 1o
53 1g 1o 1b 1w 1b 1o 1g 1o 1w 1o 1g 1o 1b 1w 1b 1o 1g
54 1o 1b 1w 1b 1o 2g 1o 1w 1o 2g 1o 1b 1w 1b 1o
55 1b 1w 1b 1o 3g 1o 1w 1o 3g 1o 1b 1w 1b
56 1w 1b 1o 4y 1o 1w 1o 4y 1o 1b 1w
57 1b 1o 1g 4y 1o 1w 1o 4y 1g 1o 1b
58 1o 2g 2y 2g 1o 1w 1o 2g 2y 2g 1o
59 1o 4y 1g 1o 1b 1bl 1b 1o 1g 4y 1o
60 1o 4y 1o 2b 1bl 2b 1o 4y 1o
61 1o 3g 1o 3b 1bl 3b 1o 3g 1o
62 1o 2g 1o 3b 1bl 1o 1bl 3b 1o 2g 1o
63 1o 1g 1o 3b 1bl 3o 1bl 3b 1o 1g 1o
64 2o 3b 1bl 5o 1bl 3b 2o

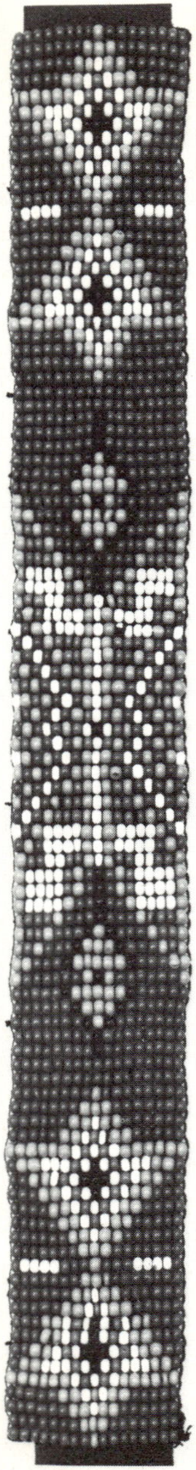

65 1o 6b 1o 1bl 1o 6b 1o
66 5b 1bl 5o 1bl 5b
67 6b 1bl 3o 1bl 6b
68 7b 1bl 1o 1bl 7b
69 8b 1bl 8b (2 rows)
71 17b (2 rows)
73 8b 1o 8b
74 7b 3o 7b
75 6b 2o 1w 2o 6b
76 5b 2o 1w 1g 1w 2o 5b
77 6o 1w 1g 1y 1g 1w 6o
78 1b 2o 3w 1g 1y 1bl 1y 1g 3w 2o 1b
79 2b 2o 1w 1g 1y 3bl 1y 1g 1w 2o 2b
80 3b 2o 1w 1g 1y 1bl 1y 1g 1w 2o 3b
81 4b 2o 1w 1g 1y 1g 1w 2o 4b
82 5b 2o 1w 1g 1w 2o 5b
83 6b 2o 1w 2o 6b
84 7b 3o 7b
85 1b 4y 3b 1o 3b 4y 1b
86 7b 3o 7b
87 6b 2o 1w 2o 6b
88 5b 2o 1w 1g 1w 2o 5b
89 4b 2o 1w 1g 1y 1g 1w 2o 4b
90 3b 2o 1w 1g 1y 1bl 1y 1g 1w 2o 3b
91 2b 2o 1w 1g 1y 3bl 1y 1g 1w 2o 2b
92 1b 2o 3w 1g 1y 1bl 1y 1g 3w 2o 1b
93 6o 1w 1g 1y 1g 1w 6o
94 5b 2o 1w 1g 1w 2o 5b
95 6b 2o 1w 2o 6b
96 7b 3o 7b
97 8b 1o 8b

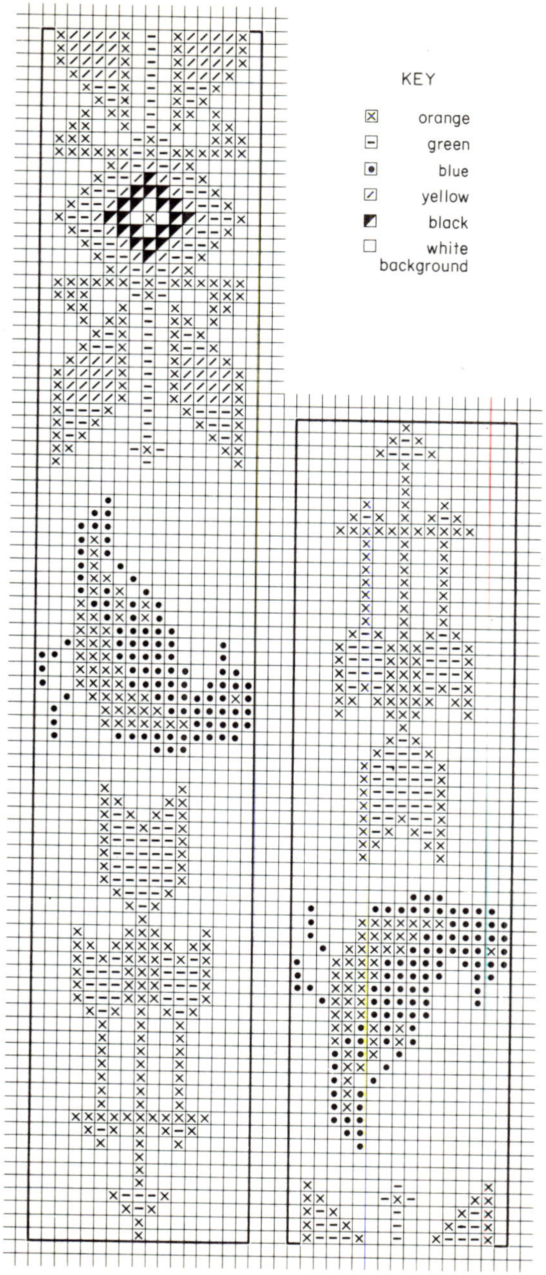

PATTERN TWENTY-NINE Strip of beadwork.

Key

w = white o = orange
g = green y = yellow
bl = black b = blue

18 warp threads 17 beads

1 8w 1o 8w (2 rows)
3 7w 1o 1g 1o 7w
4 6w 1o 3g 1o 6w
5 8w 1o 8w (3 rows)
8 5w 1o 2w 1o 2w 1o 5w
9 4w 1o 1g 1o 1w 1o 1w 1o 1g 1o 4w
10 3w 11o 3w
11 5w 1o 2w 1o 2w 1o 5w (7 rows)
18 4w 1o 1g 1o 1w 1o 1w 1o 1g 1o 4w
19 3w 1o 3g 3o 3g 1o 3w (3 rows)
22 3w 1o 1g 1o 1g 3o 1g 1o 1g 1o 3w
23 3w 2o 1w 5o 1w 2o 3w
24 3w 1o 3w 3o 3w 1o 3w
25 8w 1o 8w
26 7w 1o 1g 1o 7w
27 6w 1o 3g 1o 6w
28 5w 1o 5g 1o 5w (4 rows)
32 5w 1o 2g 1o 2g 1o 5w
33 5w 1o 1g 1o 1w 1o 1g 1o 5w
34 5w 2o 3w 2o 5w
35 5w 1o 5w 1o 5w
36 17w (2 rows)
38 9w 3b 5w

39 1w 1b 4w 10b 1w
40 1w 1b 3w 7o 5b
41 1w 1b 3w 5o 7b
42 2w 1b 1w 5o 6b 1o 1b
43 1b 2w 4o 5b 1w 4b
44 1b 2w 4o 5b 2w 2b 1w
45 2b 1w 3o 5b 3w 1b 2w
46 2w 1b 3o 5b 3w 1b 2w
47 3w 3o 5b 6w
48 3w 2o 1b 1o 1b 1o 1b 7w
49 3w 1o 2b 1o 1b 1o 1b 7w
50 3w 1b 1o 1b 1o 1w 1b 8w
51 3w 1b 2o 1w 1b 9w
52 3w 1b 1o 1w 1b 10w
53 3w 1b 1o 1b 11w (2 rows)
55 3w 3b 11w
56 4w 2b 11w
57 5w 1b 11w
58 17w (2 rows)
60 1w 1o 6w 1g 6w 1o 1w
61 1w 2o 4w 1g 1o 1g 4w 2o 1w
62 1w 1o 1g 1o 4w 1g 4w 1o 1g 1o 1w
63 1w 1o 2g 1o 3w 1g 3w 1o 2g 1o 1w
64 1w 1o 3g 1o 2w 1g 2w 1o 3g 1o 1w
65 1w 1o 4y 1o 1w 1g 1w 1o 4y 1o 1w (3 rows)
68 2w 1o 3y 1o 1w 1g 1w 1o 3y 1o 2w
69 3w 1o 2g 1o 1w 1g 1w 1o 2g 1o 3w
70 4w 1o 1g 1o 1w 1g 1w 1o 1g 1o 4w
71 3w 1o 1w 2o 1w 1g 1w 2o 1w 1o 3w
72 2w 2o 2w 1o 1w 1g 1w 1o 2w 2o 2w
73 1w 3o 3w 1g 1o 1g 3w 3o 1w
74 1w 6o 1g 1o 1g 6o 1w
75 5w 1o 1y 1g 1y 1g 1y 1o 5w
76 4w 1o 2g 1y 1bl 1y 2g 1o 4w
77 3w 1o 2g 1y 3bl 1y 2g 1o 3w
78 2w 1o 2g 1y 2bl 1w 2bl 1y 2g 1o 2w
79 1w 1o 2g 1y 2bl 1w 1o 1w 2bl 1y 2g 1o 1w
80 2w 1o 2g 1y 2bl 1w 2bl 1y 2g 1o 2w
81 3w 1o 2g 1y 3bl 1y 2g 1o 3w
82 4w 1o 2g 1y 1bl 1y 2g 1o 4w
83 5w 1o 1y 1g 1y 1g 1y 1o 5w
84 1w 6o 1g 1o 1g 6o 1w
85 1w 3o 3w 1g 1o 1g 3w 3o 1w
86 2w 2o 2w 1o 1w 1g 1w 1o 2w 2o 2w
87 3w 1o 1w 2o 1w 1g 1w 2o 1w 1o 3w
88 4w 1o 1g 1o 1w 1g 1w 1o 1g 1o 4w
89 3w 1o 2g 1o 1w 1g 1w 1o 2g 1o 3w
90 2w 1o 3y 1o 1w 1g 1w 1o 3y 1o 2w
91 1w 1o 4y 1o 1w 1g 1w 1o 4y 1o 1w (3 rows)
94 1w 1o 3g 1o 2w 1g 2w 1o 3g 1o 1w
95 1w 1o 2g 1o 3w 1g 3w 1o 2g 1o 1w
96 1w 1o 1g 1o 4w 1g 4w 1o 1g 1o 1w
97 1w 2o 4w 1g 1o 1g 4w 2o 1w
98 1w 1o 6w 1g 6w 1o 1w
99 17w (2 rows)
Repeat Rows 57 to 1 working in reverse (e.g. 57, 56, 55 etc.)

(*opposite*): Pattern 29. Strip of beadwork showing the handwoven ends before attaching *Velcro* or mounting

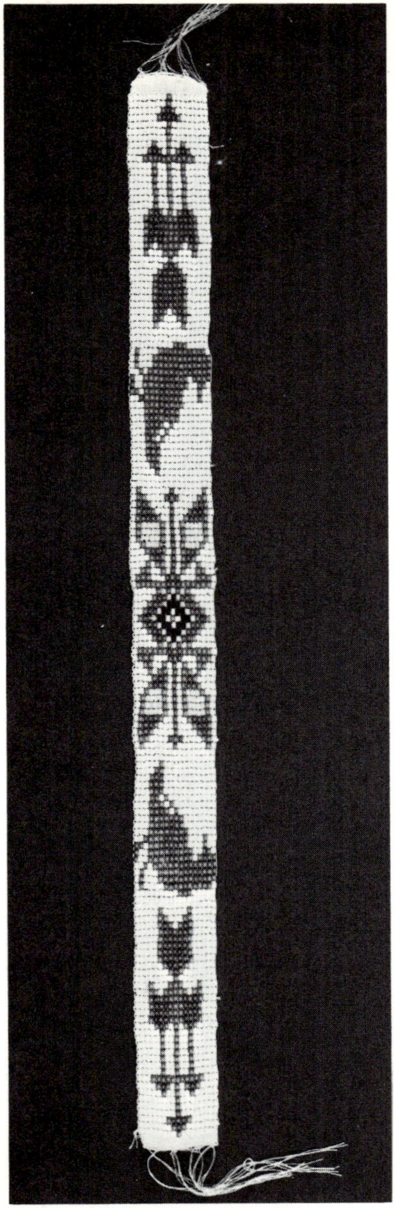

PATTERN THIRTY For a choker 305 mm (12 in.) long.

Key
b = blue background
bl = black o = orange
w = white

18 warp threads 17 beads
1 17b (repeat for 17 rows)
18 8b 1w 8b
19 7b 1w 1bl 1w 7b
20 6b 1w 3bl 1w 6b
21 5b 1w 5bl 1w 5b
22 4b 1w 7bl 1w 4b
23 3b 1w 9bl 1w 3b
24 2b 1w 11bl 1w 2b
25 1b 1w 13bl 1w 1b
26 1w 7bl 1o 7bl 1w
27 1b 1w 5bl 1o 1w 1o 5bl 1w 1b
28 2b 1w 3bl 1o 3w 1o 3bl 1w 2b
29 3b 1w 1bl 1o 5w 1o 1bl 1w 3b
30 4b 1o 7w 1o 4b
31 3b 1o 9w 1o 3b
32 2b 1o 11w 1o 2b
33 1b 1o 13w 1o 1b
34 1o 7w 1bl 7w 1o
35 1b 1o 5w 1bl 1o 1bl 5w 1o 1b
36 2b 1o 3w 1bl 3o 1bl 3w 1o 2b
37 3b 1o 1w 1bl 5o 1bl 1w 1o 3b
38 4b 1bl 7o 1bl 4b
39 3b 1bl 9o 1bl 3b
40 2b 1bl 11o 1bl 2b
41 1b 1bl 13o 1bl 1b

Commence side fringing (see Chapter 6.)

42 1bl 15o 1bl 38b (38b for first strand of fringe)
43 1b 1bl 13o 1bl 39b
44 2b 1bl 11o 1bl 40b
45 3b 1bl 9o 1bl 41b
46 4b 1bl 7o 1bl 42b
47 5b 1bl 5o 1bl 43b
48 6b 1bl 3o 1bl 44b
49 7b 1bl 1o 1bl 45b
50 8b 1bl 46b
51 8b 1o 46b
52 7b 3o 45b
53 6b 2o 1b 2o 44b
54 5b 2o 3b 2o 43b
55 4b 2o 5b 2o 42b
56 3b 2o 7b 2o 41b
57 2b 2o 9b 2o 40b
58 1b 2o 11b 2o 39b
59 2o 6b 1w 6b 2o 38b
60 1b 2o 4b 3w 4b 2o 39b
61 2b 2o 2b 2w 1b 2w 2b 2o 40b
62 3b 2o 2w 3b 2w 2o 41b
63 4b 2o 5b 2o 42b
64 3b 2w 2o 3b 2o 2w 41b
65 2b 2w 2b 2o 1b 2o 2b 2w 40b
66 1b 2w 4b 3o 4b 2w 39b
67 2w 6b 1w 6b 2w 38b
68 1b 2w 4b 3bl 4b 2w 39b
69 2b 2w 2b 2bl 1b 2bl 2b 2w 40b

70 3b 2w 2bl 3b 2bl 2w 41b
71 4b 2bl 5b 2bl 42b
72 3b 2bl 2w 3b 2w 2bl 41b
73 2b 2bl 2b 2w 1b 2w 2b 2bl 40b
74 1b 2bl 4b 3w 4b 2bl 39b
75 2bl 6b 1w 6b 2bl 38b
76 1b 2bl 11b 2bl 39b
77 2b 2bl 9b 2bl 40b
78 3b 2bl 7b 2bl 41b
79 4b 2bl 5b 2bl 42b
80 5b 2bl 3b 2bl 43b
81 6b 2bl 1b 2bl 44b
82 7b 3bl 45b
83 8b 1bl 46b
84 8b 1w 46b
85 7b 1w 1bl 1w 45b
86 6b 1w 3bl 1w 44b
87 5b 1w 5bl 1w 43b
88 4b 1w 7bl 1w 42b
89 3b 1w 9bl 1w 41b
90 2b 1w 11bl 1w 40b
91 1b 1w 13bl 1w 39b
92 1w 7bl 1o 7bl 1w 38b

End of fringe

93 1b 1w 5bl 1o 1w 1o 5bl 1w 1b
94 2b 1w 3bl 1o 3w 1o 3bl 1w 2b
95 3b 1w 1bl 1o 5w 1o 1bl 1w 3b
96 4b 1o 7w 1o 4b
97 3b 1o 9w 1o 3b
98 2b 1o 11w 1o 2b
99 1b 1o 13w 1o 1b
100 1o 15w 1o
101 1b 1o 5w 1bl 1o 1bl 5w 1o 1b
102 2b 1o 3w 1bl 3o 1bl 3w 1o 2b
103 3b 1o 1w 1bl 5o 1bl 1w 1o 3b
104 4b 1bl 7o 1bl 4b
105 3b 1bl 9o 1bl 3b
106 2b 1bl 11o 1bl 2b
107 1b 1bl 13o 1bl 1b
108 1bl 15o 1bl
109 1b 1bl 13o 1bl 1b
110 2b 1bl 11o 1bl 2b
111 3b 1bl 9o 1bl 3b
112 4b 1bl 7o 1bl 4b
113 5b 1bl 5o 1bl 5b
114 6b 1bl 3o 1bl 6b
115 7b 1bl 1o 1bl 7b
116 8b 1bl 8b
117 17b (17 rows)

To finish the ends, see Chapter 6.

Pattern 30: Choker showing side fringing

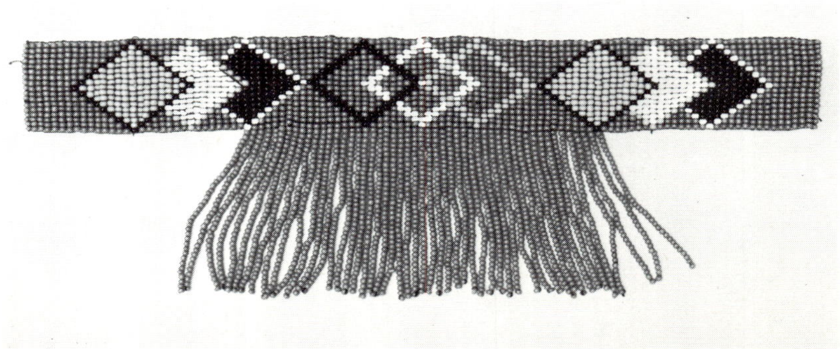

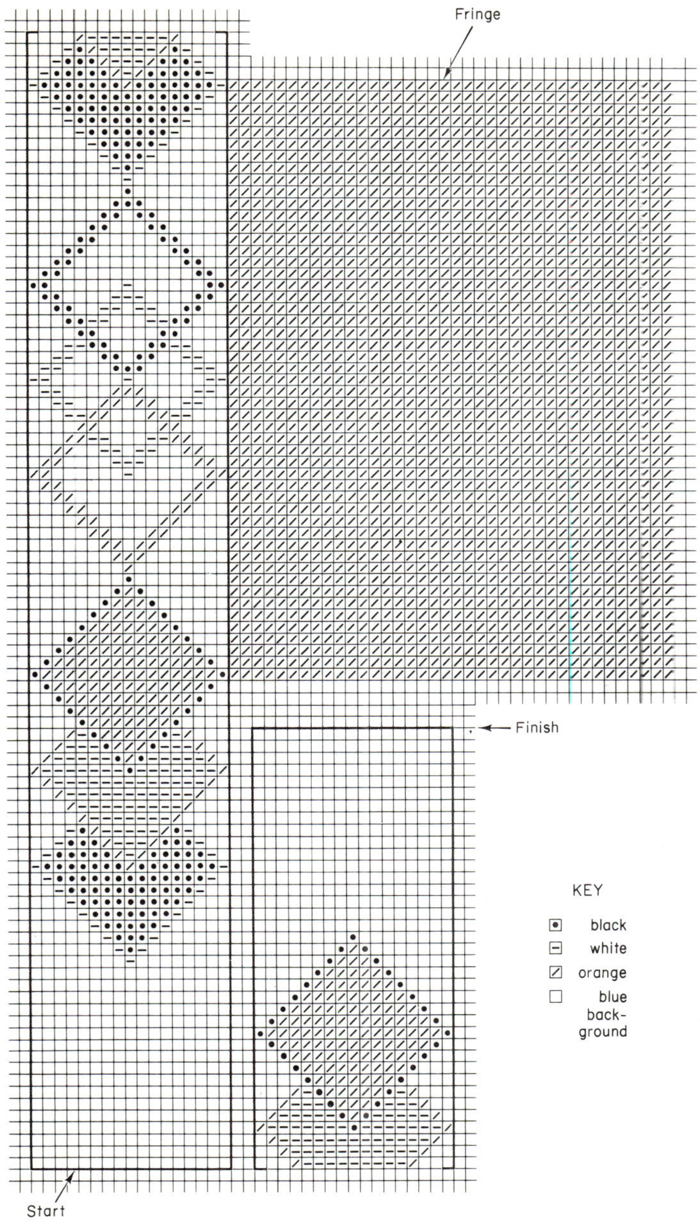

The graph shows a fringe in a contrasting colour

PATTERN THIRTY-ONE Fringed bracelet.

This graph shows one half of the bracelet. On completion of row 33, work back down the graph, ending at row 1

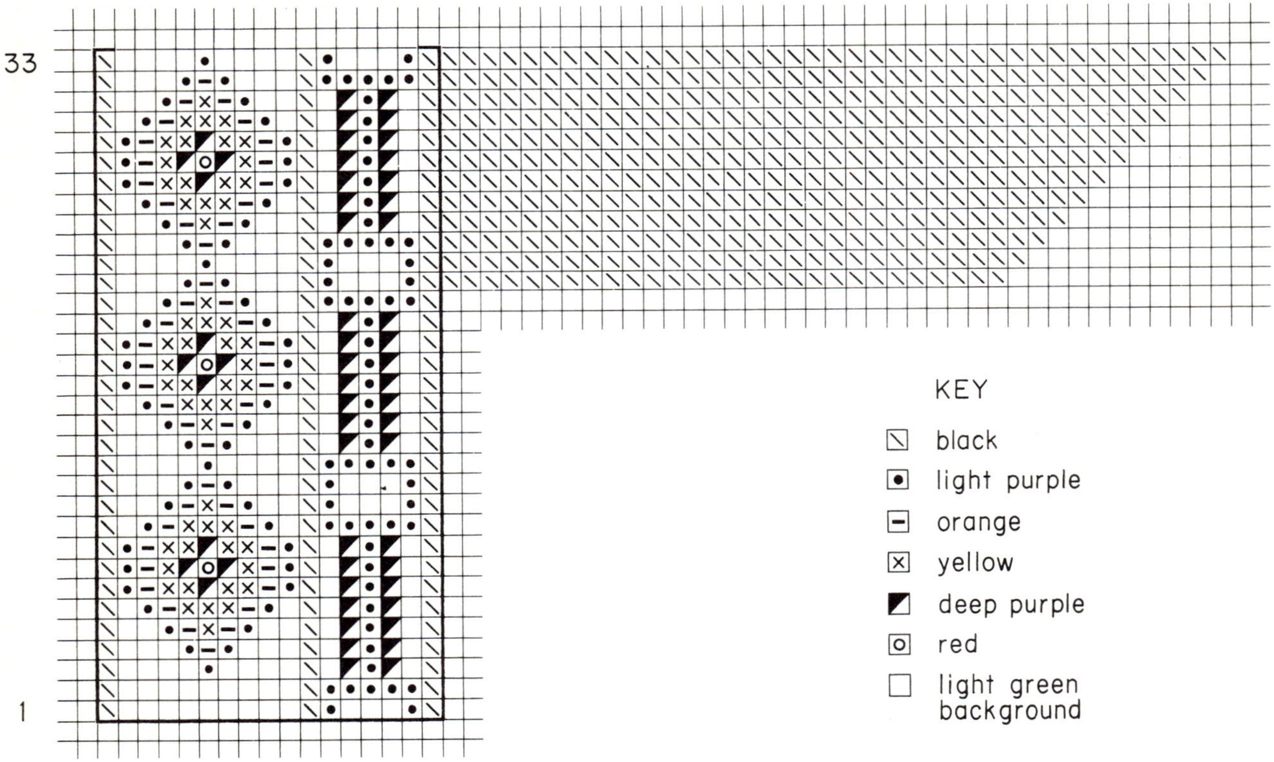

Key

- ● = light purple (lp)
- — = orange (o)
- × = yellow (y)
- ◤ = deep purple (p)
- ○ = red (r)
- \ = black (b)
- □ = light green (g)

18 warp threads 17 beads

1 1b 9g 1b 1lp 3g 1lp 1b

2 1b 9g 1b 5lp 1b

3 1b 4g 1lp 4g 1b 1g 1p 1lp 1p 1g 1b

4 1b 3g 1lp 1o 1lp 3g 1b 1g 1p 1lp 1p 1g 1b

5 1b 2g 1lp 1o 1y 1o 1lp 2g 1b 1g 1p 1lp 1p 1g 1b

6 1b 1g 1lp 1o 3y 1o 1lp 1g 1b 1g 1p 1lp 1p 1g 1b

7 1b 1lp 1o 2y 1p 2y 1o 1lp 1b 1g 1p 1lp 1p 1g 1b

8 1b 1lp 1o 1y 1p 1r 1p 1y 1o 1lp 1b 1g 1p 1lp 1p 1g 1b

9 1b 1lp 1o 2y 1p 2y 1o 1lp 1b 1g 1p 1lp 1p 1g 1b

10 1b 1g 1lp 1o 3y 1o 1lp 1g 1b 5lp 1b

11 1b 2g 1lp 1o 1y 1o 1lp 2g 1b 1lp 3g 1lp 1b

12 1b 3g 1lp 1o 1lp 3g 1b 1lp 3g 1lp 1b

13 1b 4g 1lp 4g 1b 5lp 1b

14 1b 3g 1lp 1o 1lp 3g 1b 1g 1p 1lp 1p 1g 1b

15 1b 2g 1lp 1o 1y 1o 1lp 2g 1b 1g 1p 1lp 1p 1g 1b

16 1b 1g 1lp 1o 3y 1o 1lp 1g 1b 1g 1p 1lp 1p 1g 1b

17 1b 1lp 1o 2y 1p 2y 1o 1lp 1b 1g 1p 1lp 1p 1g 1b

18 1b 1lp 1o 1y 1p 1r 1p 1y 1o 1lp 1b 1g 1p 1lp 1p 1g 1b

19 1b 1lp 1o 2y 1p 2y 1o 1lp 1b 1g 1p 1lp 1p 1g 1b

20 1b 1g 1lp 1o 3y 1o 1lp 1g 1b 1g 1p 1lp 1p 1g 1b

21 1b 2g 1lp 1o 1y 1o 1lp 2g 1b 5lp 1b

Commence the side fringing, see Chapter 6.

22 1b 3g 1lp 1o 1lp 3g 1b 1lp 3g 1lp 29b

23 1b 4g 1lp 4g 1b 1lp 3g 1lp 30b

24 1b 3g 1lp 1o 1lp 3g 1b 5lp 31b

25 1b 2g 1lp 1o 1y 1o 1lp 2g 1b 1g 1p 1lp 1p 1g 32b

26 1b 1g 1lp 1o 3y 1o 1lp 1g 1b 1g 1p 1lp 1p 1g 33b

27 1b 1lp 1o 2y 1p 2y 1o 1lp 1b 1g 1p 1lp 1p 1g 34b

28 1b 1lp 1o 1y 1p 1r 1p 1y 1o 1lp 1b 1g 1p 1lp 1p 1g 35b

29 1b 1lp 1o 2y 1p 2y 1o 1lp 1b 1g 1p 1lp 1p 1g 36b

30 1b 1g 1lp 1o 3y 1o 1lp 1g 1b 1g 1p 1lp 1p 1g 37b

31 1b 2g 1lp 1o 1y 1o 1lp 2g 1b 1g 1p 1lp 1p 1g 38b

32 1b 3g 1lp 1o 1lp 3g 1b 5lp 39b

33 1b 4g 1lp 4g 1b 1lp 3g 1lp 40b

34 1b 3g 1lp 1o 1lp 3g 1b 1lp 3g 1lp 39b

35 1b 2g 1lp 1o 1y 1o 1lp 2g 1b 5lp 38b

36 1b 1g 1lp 1o 3y 1o 1lp 1g 1b 1g 1p 1lp 1p 1g 37b

37 1b 1lp 1o 2y 1p 2y 1o 1lp 1b 1g 1p 1lp 1p 1g 36b

38 1b 1lp 1o 1y 1p 1r 1p 1y 1o 1lp 1b 1g 1p 1lp 1p 1g 35b

39 1b 1lp 1o 2y 1p 2y 1o 1lp 1b 1g 1p 1lp 1p 1g 34b

40 1b 1g 1lp 1o 3y 1o 1lp 1g 1b 1g 1p 1lp 1p 1g 33b

41 1b 2g 1lp 1o 1y 1o 1lp 2g 1b 1g 1p 1lp 1p 1g 32b

42 1b 3g 1lp 1o 1lp 3g 1b 1g 1p 1lp 1p 1g 31b

43 1b 4g 1lp 4g 1b 5lp 30b

44 1b 3g 1lp 1o 1lp 3g 1b 1lp 3g 1lp 29b

45 1b 2g 1lp 1o 1y 1o 1lp 2g 1b 1lp 3g 1lp 1b

46 1b 1g 1lp 1o 3y 1o 1lp 1g 1b 5lp 1b

47 1b 1lp 1o 2y 1p 2y 1o 1lp 1b 1g 1p 1lp 1p 1g 1b

48 1b 1lp 1o 1y 1p 1r 1p 1y 1o 1lp 1b 1g 1p 1lp 1p 1g 1b

49 1b 1lp 1o 2y 1p 2y 1o 1lp 1b 1g 1p 1lp 1p 1g 1b

50 1b 1g 1lp 1o 3y 1o 1lp 1g 1b 1g 1p 1lp 1p 1g 1b

51 1b 2g 1lp 1o 1y 1o 1lp 2g 1b 1g 1p 1lp 1p 1g 1b

52 1b 3g 1lp 1o 1lp 3g 1b 1g 1p 1lp 1p 1g 1b

53 1b 4g 1lp 4g 1b 1g 1p 1lp 1p 1g 1b

54 1b 3g 1lp 1o 1lp 3g 1b 5lp 1b

55 1b 2g 1lp 1o 1y 1o 1lp 2g 1b 1lp 3g 1lp 1b

56 1b 1g 1lp 1o 3y 1o 1lp 1g 1b 1lp 3g 1lp 1b

57 1b 1lp 1o 2y 1p 2y 1o 1lp 1b 5lp 1b

58 1b 1lp 1o 1y 1p 1r 1p 1y

1o 1lp 1b 1g 1p 1lp 1p
1g 1b
59 1b 1lp 1o 2y 1p 2y 1o 1lp
1b 1g 1p 1lp 1p 1g 1b
60 1b 1g 1lp 1o 3y 1o 1lp 1g
1b 1g 1p 1lp 1p 1g 1b
61 1b 2g 1lp 1o 1y 1o 1lp 2g
1b 1g 1p 1lp 1p 1g 1b
62 1b 3g 1lp 1o 1lp 3g 1b 1g
1p 1lp 1p 1g 1b
63 1b 4g 1lp 4g 1b 1g 1p 1lp
1p 1g 1b
64 1b 9g 1b 1g 1p 1lp 1p 1g
1b
65 1b 9g 1b 5lp 1b

For finishing ends, see Chapter 6.

Pattern 31: Bracelet with side fringing

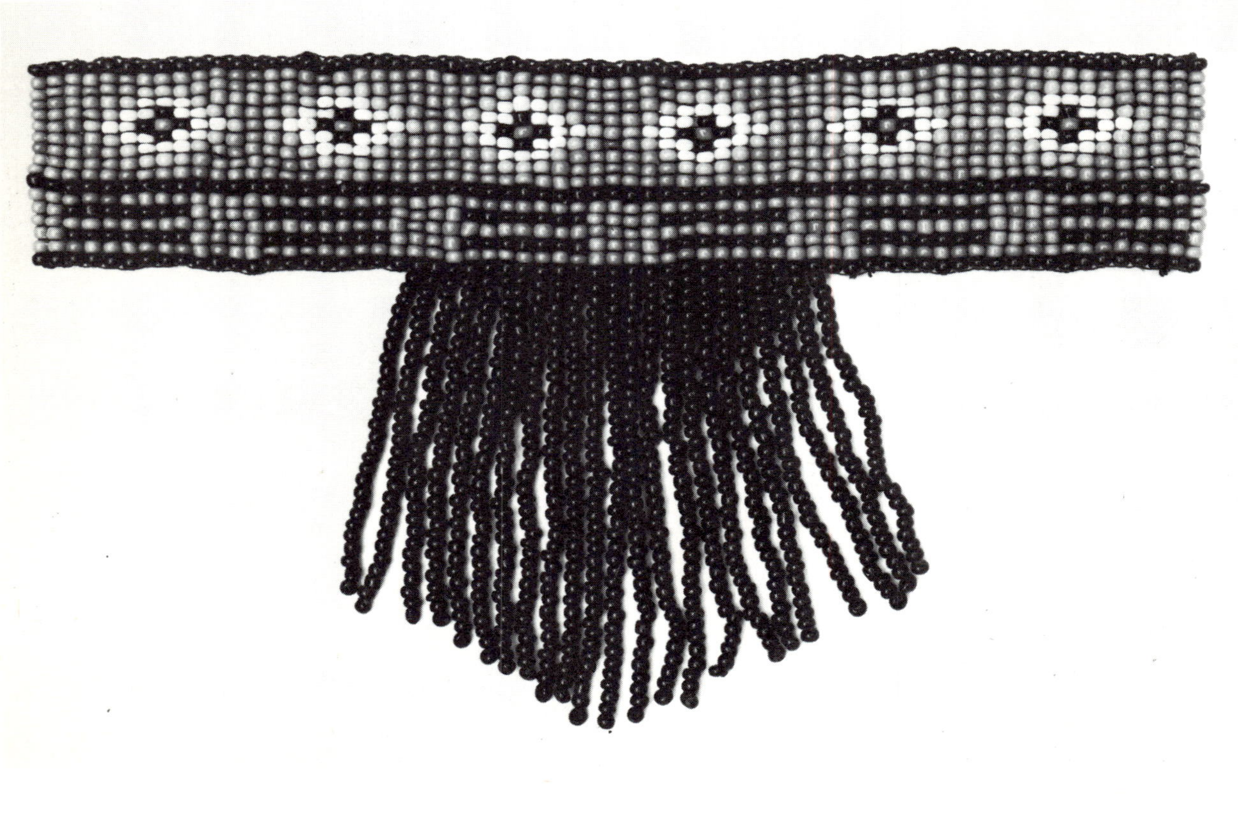

8 Beadwork for dressmakers

All the beadwork patterns in Chapters 1 and 2 are ideal for delicate edgings around necklines and sleeve edges. Before attaching the strips of beadwork permanently, always test a small strip to see how it washes. Good quality beads should not lose their colour in water.

The collar designs in Chapter 2 make a particularly attractive edging for a neckline, and can enhance an evening dress when worked in pearl, gold, or silver beads.

It is interesting to note that the same pattern worked in a different colour or size can give an entirely different effect. For instance, the collar designs in Chapter 2, worked in navy and pearl, look much more delicate than those worked in red and white beads.

BEADWORK WORKED ON THE LOOM

All the patterns in Chapter 7 can be used as insertions in dressmaking. A strip sewn onto a cuff or round a neckline can transform a plain, ordinary dress into something special.

A tunic top with contrasting strips of beadwork inserted into the side seams looks attractive, and a piece of beadwork running down the centre of a shirt dress fits particularly well. The following design worked in white and gold was recently used on the edging of a long coat to wear over a wedding-dress.

Key

□ = white background

● = gold

10 warp threads 9 beads

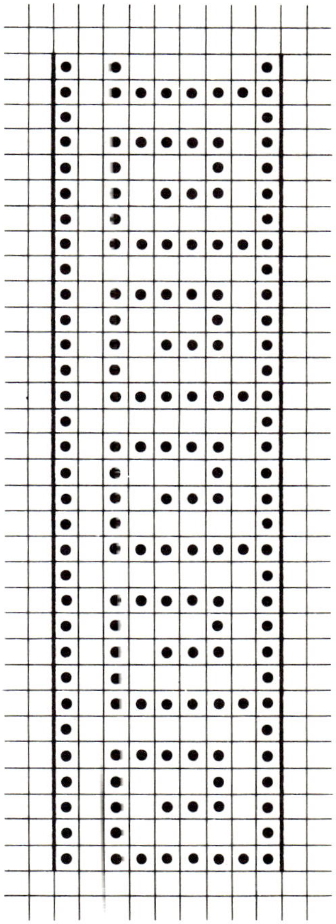

APPLIQUE WORK USING BEADS

Creating your own individual designs on clothing, soft leather, bags, and mocassins is extremely simple, and the results are rewarding.

Using tailor's chalk, sketch out your design, and then commence beading as described below.

APPLIQUE STITCH BEADING

Take a thread of beads and sew them onto the cloth. Using a second needle, and a double, waxed thread, catch the beading thread between every second or third bead. This method is used by North American Indians for their floral design beadwork.

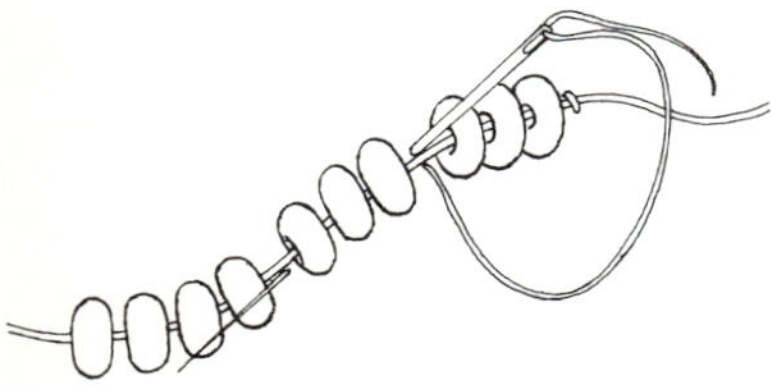

For circular designs and small details the following method is more suitable.

Find the centre of the design, and sew on a centre bead. Sew down each bead in the row surrounding this centre bead.

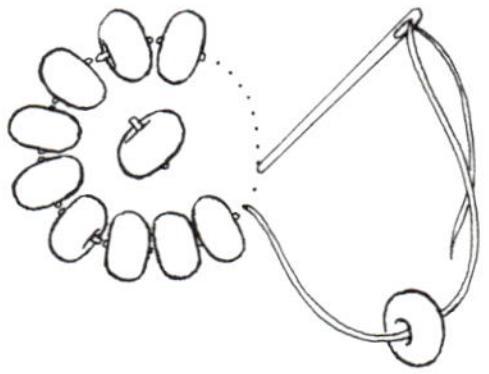

Now stitch down four beads at a time in the following way: Thread four beads and pass the needle down through the fabric. Now bring the needle back up between the second and third beads. Thread the needle through the third and fourth bead for the second time.

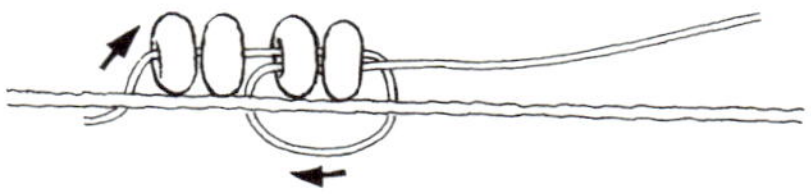

After each row is sewn down, run the thread through the entire row of beads, once more, to even them up.

Continue until the circle is filled.

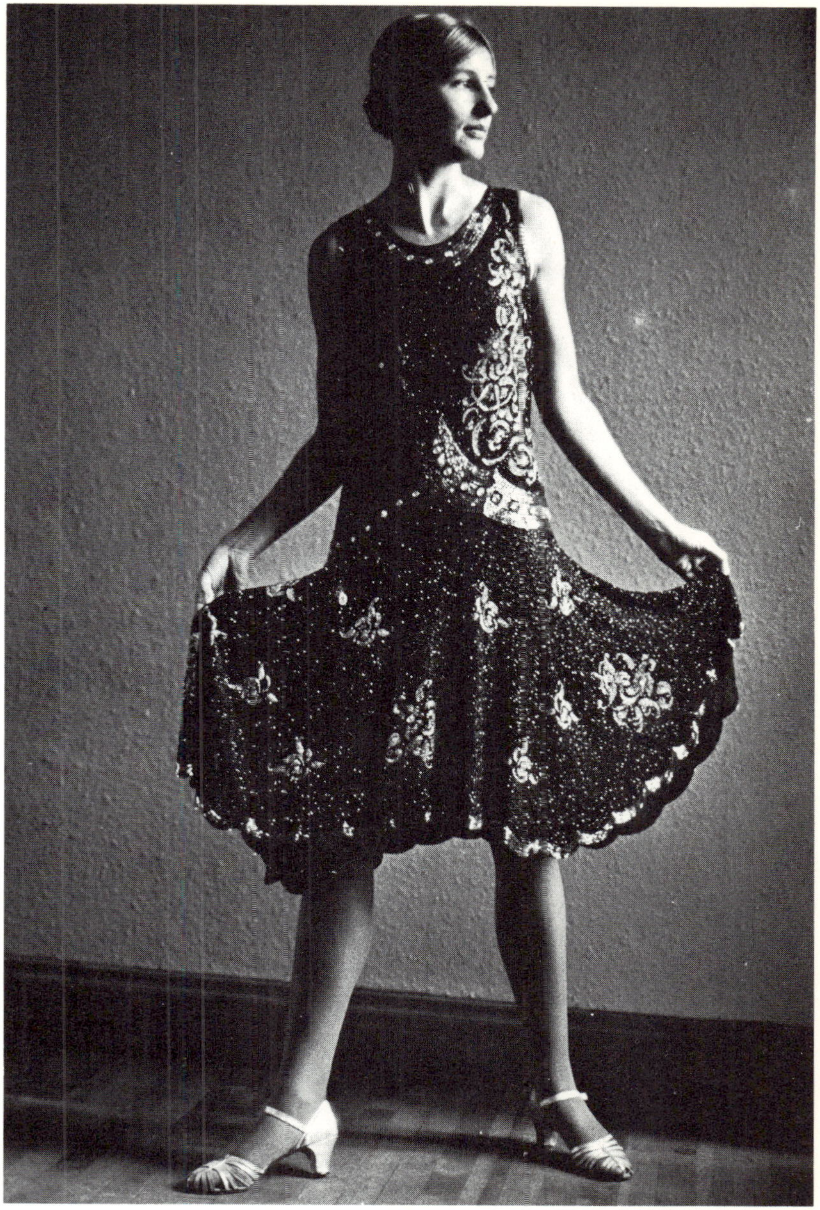

An early 20th-century French beaded dress

9 Designing your own work

Beginners will find it easier to follow a chart, but after a little practice will be able to work a design without having to follow a pattern.

Make a chart yourself on graph paper. Each square will represent one bead. Colour the squares, according to your design, with felt-tipped pens. Start with a simple repeating design for a belt or a choker.

When creating a design for beadwork, remember that curved lines have to be built up row by row.

The number of warp threads used is in accordance with the width required for the finished beadwork. In Chapter 7, 22 to 26 warp threads were used for the necklaces and 12 to 18 warp threads for the strips of beadwork.

In the example shown the graphed design has been written in the same form as a knitting pattern. One will observe that the rows are numbered from the bottom of the graphed design, and the same numbers relate to each row of the written pattern.

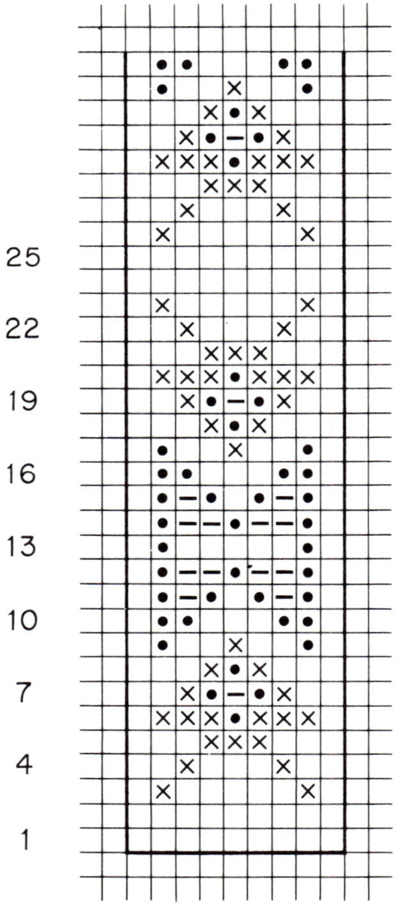

Strip of beadwork
(To be used for inserts in dressmaking, or for a belt, choker, or bracelet.)

Key

= white background (w)
× = black (bl)
● = orange (o)
— = blue (b)

Here is the graph converted to a beading pattern.

10 warp threads 9 beads
1 9w (2 rows)
3 1w 1bl 5w 1bl 1w
4 2w 1bl 3w 1bl 2w
5 3w 3bl 3w
6 1w 3bl 1o 3bl 1w
7 2w 1bl 1o 1b 1o 1bl 2w
8 3w 1bl 1o 1bl 3w
9 1w 1o 2w 1bl 2w 1o 1w
10 1w 2o 3w 2o 1w
11 1w 1o 1b 1o 1w 1o 1b 1o 1w
12 1w 1o 2b 1o 2b 1o 1w
13 1w 1o 5w 1o 1w
14 1w 1o 2b 1o 2b 1o 1w
15 1w 1o 1b 1o 1w 1o 1b 1o 1w
16 1w 2o 3w 2o 1w
17 1w 1o 2w 1bl 2w 1o 1w
18 3w 1bl 1o 1bl 3w
19 2w 1bl 1o 1w 1o 1bl 2w
20 1w 3bl 1o 3bl 1w
21 3w 3bl 3w
22 2w 1bl 3w 1bl 2w
23 1w 1bl 5w 1bl 1w

Repeat rows 1 to 23 for the desired length.
To finish ends, see Chapter 6.

Suppliers

Great Britain

All the firms listed supply the full range of necessary materials unless it is stated otherwise. All offer mail order facilities.

LONDON

The Needlewoman Shop
146–148 Regent Street
London W1 6BA

Ells and Farrier Ltd
5 Princes Street
Hanover Square
London W1

THE NORTH

Fred Aldous Ltd
37 Lever Street
Manchester 1

Thomas Hope Ltd
Educational Suppliers
St Philip's Drive
Royton, Oldham
Lancashire

THE SOUTH

Murphy Industries
PO Box 44
Portsmouth PO1 2TH
Hampshire

Canada

Tandy Leather Company
1224 Rue Drummond
Montreal 107
P Quebec

Branches are also to be found in sixteen major cities across the country. Consult the 'Yellow Pages' of the telephone directory.

House of Orange
3621 West Broadway
Vancouver 8
British Columbia

This company stocks beads only, but has an excellent, exciting selection.

USA

American Handicrafts Co

This company has 56 stores from coast to coast, in most major cities. Consult the 'Yellow Pages' for your nearest branch.

EAST COAST

Boutique Craft Inc
Box 23-M
New Hyde Park
New York, NY 11040

Sheru Bead Boutique Shop
49 West 38th Street
New York, NY 10018

Nicole Bead & Craft Co Inc
924 Cherry Street
Philadelphia, Pennsylvania 19107

WEST COAST

Bead Game
505 North Fairfax Avenue
Los Angeles, California 90036

Bethlehem Imports
5231 Cushman Place
San Diego, California 92110

Gloria's Glass Garden
Box 1990
Beverley Hills, California 90213

Kit Kraft
12109 Ventura Place
Studio City
California 91604

SOUTH

The Beadcraft Corner
PO Box 5754
Augusta Georgia 30906